DINOSAURS

MICHAEL BENTON

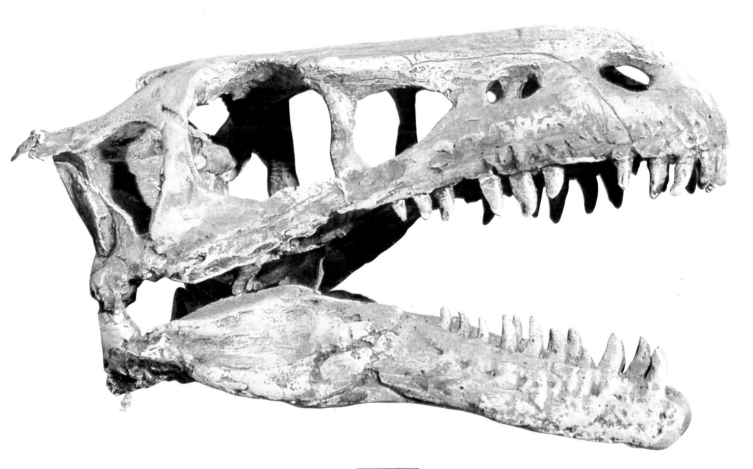

SMITHMARK

The Author

Michael Benton, lecturer in palaeontology at the University of Bristol, England, has loved dinosaurs since he was seven. He has worked on scientific problems concerning the origin of the dinosaurs, their evolution, and their extinction, and has published numerous scientific papers. Right now, he is working on new finds of fossil reptiles, including dinosaurs, from the Triassic of Devon, England and Morayshire, Scotland, as well as from the Jurassic of Gloucestershire, England.

He has written 14 books on dinosaurs and other aspects of the history of life, including *Dinosaurs, an A-Z guide* and *Prehistoric animals, an A-Z guide* (both Derrydale), *All about dinosaurs* (Mallard Press), *On the trail of the dinosaurs, The reign of the reptiles*, and *The rise of the mammals* (all Crescent Books). His textbook, *Vertebrate Palaeontology* (Chapman & Hall) came out in 1990.

Editor:
Philip de Ste. Croix

Design:
Stonecastle Graphics Ltd

Picture Research:
Leora Kahn

Production:
Ruth Arthur
Sally Connolly
Neil Randles

Filmset:
SX Composing

Colour Reproduction:
Advance Laser Graphic Arts, Hong Kong

CLB 2606

This edition published in 1995 by SMITHMARK Publishers, a division of U.S. Media Holdings, Inc., 16 East 32nd Street, New York NY 10016

SMITHMARK books are available for bulk purchase for sales promotion and premium use. For details write or call the manager of special sales, SMITHMARK Publishers, Inc., 16 East 32nd Street, New York, NY 10016; (212) 532-6600

Produced by CLB Publishing, Godalming Business Centre
Woolsack Way, Godalming, Surrey, UK
ISBN 0-8317-5368-4
Printed in Italy

CONTENTS

1 Setting the Scene

Dinosaurs lived on Earth long ago, during the Mesozoic Era, which is often known as the "Age of the Dinosaurs". The dinosaurs lived for 160 million years, eventually dying out 65 million years ago, long before the origin of humans 5 million years ago.

These vast amounts of time, measured in millions of years, have been based upon studies of rocks by geologists. Long ago, geologists realised that the Earth was very ancient, and that vast thicknesses of rocks have been deposited, with the oldest layers generally at the bottom of the pile. Exact ages of the rocks are found out by studies of rocks that have natural radioactivity. Radioactive elements are not stable, and they decay, or change, over time into other elements. The rates of decay are known, and it is possible to estimate the exact age of a rock sample by comparing the amount of a radioactive element left and the amount of the end product.

Fossils are also used in dating, and they can give quick and accurate age estimates, but not in millions of years. Fossils are the remains of once-living plants and animals which have been preserved in the rock. There is a very rich fossil record in the rocks, thousands of species having been preserved through the past 3,500 million years. The fossils give evidence for change through time, or *evolution*. Different groups come and go at specific times, and rocks of any particular age may contain specific fossils that are never found in rocks of any other age.

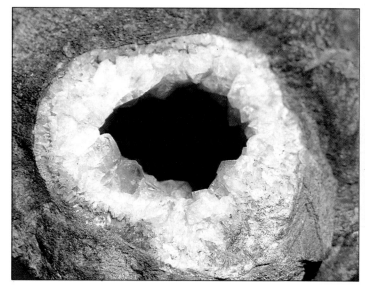

Above: A microscopic section of dinosaur bone shows complex mineral replacement, calcite in the centre, and pale amethyst elsewhere.

Right: *Eryops*, a large amphibian known from the Early Permian of Texas, and other parts of the midwestern U.S.A. This hefty meat-eater has a heavy skeleton, a massive broad-mouthed skull, and sprawling legs.

Right: The history of the Earth stretches back about 4,600 million years: more than four and a half billion years! Common fossils are known only in the last 600 million years. This span of time has been divided up by scientists into a number of geological Eras and Periods, and ages can be measured.

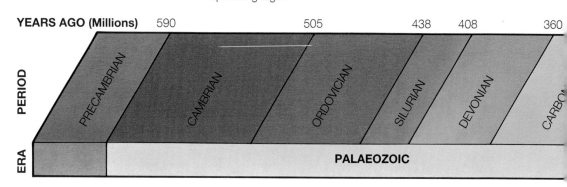

YEARS AGO (Millions)	590	505	438	408	360
PERIOD	PRECAMBRIAN	CAMBRIAN	ORDOVICIAN	SILURIAN	DEVONIAN	CARBO
ERA		PALAEOZOIC			

Fossil evidence, and exact age dating, form the basis of the geological time scale, an international standard. Time is divided into Eons, Eras, and Periods, and these may be further divided up into smaller units. This is a useful reference for geologists in all countries, and it is the time scale that is used to calibrate the evolution of life. The dinosaurs arose in the Late Triassic Period, ruled the Earth during the Jurassic and Cretaceous, and died out at the Cretaceous-Tertiary boundary.

Above: A scene in the great coal forests of North America during Carboniferous times, showing huge trees.

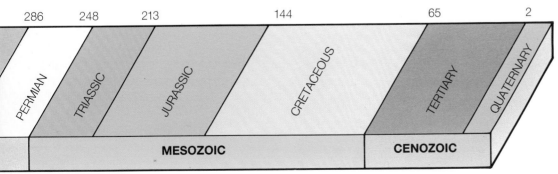

286	248	213		144		65		2
PERMIAN	TRIASSIC	JURASSIC		CRETACEOUS		TERTIARY		QUATERNARY
	MESOZOIC					**CENOZOIC**		

Above: A skeleton of the small lightly built marine reptile *Pachypleurosaurus*, known from the Middle Triassic of Central Europe. This is a nothosaur, a group of long-necked reptiles which fed on fishes. This creature was a contemporary of the early dinosaurs, but not a dinosaur itself.

2 The Triassic

The first dinosaurs inhabited a warmer world than the one we live in today. As far as we know, there was no ice at the north pole or the south pole, and this meant that temperatures around the globe were higher. Plants were different in many ways from the typical modern forms. There were no grasses, and no flowering plants of any kind. The only trees were conifers, like spruces, pines, cypresses and monkeypuzzles, and exotic maidenhair ferns and seedferns, an extinct group.

The best-known early dinosaurs come from Europe and North America. In Germany, for example, some 220 million years ago, the scene was dominated by dinosaurs large and small. The 5 metre- (16ft-) long plant-eater *Plateosaurus* fed on plants at ground level, and also browsed in the tree tops. It had a large curved thumb claw that may have been used to rake in leaves to its mouth.

The meat-eaters of these early dinosaur days were small: *Procompsognathus* and *Halticosaurus* were of about human height, but much more lightly built. Clearly, they could not have fed on *Plateosaurus*, which was much too big. They must have preyed on the smaller animals that were around at that time: frogs, turtles, lizard-like sphenodontids and early mammals.

Above: Reconstruction of *Plateosaurus*, the earliest large dinosaur. It fed on plants and used the large thumb claw to drag in food, which it cut up with its sharp teeth.

Left: Footprints called *Cheirotherium*, which were made by a meat-eating rauisuchian in the Middle Triassic sediments of central Europe. These were quadrupedal animals, unlike the essentially bipedal dinosaurs.

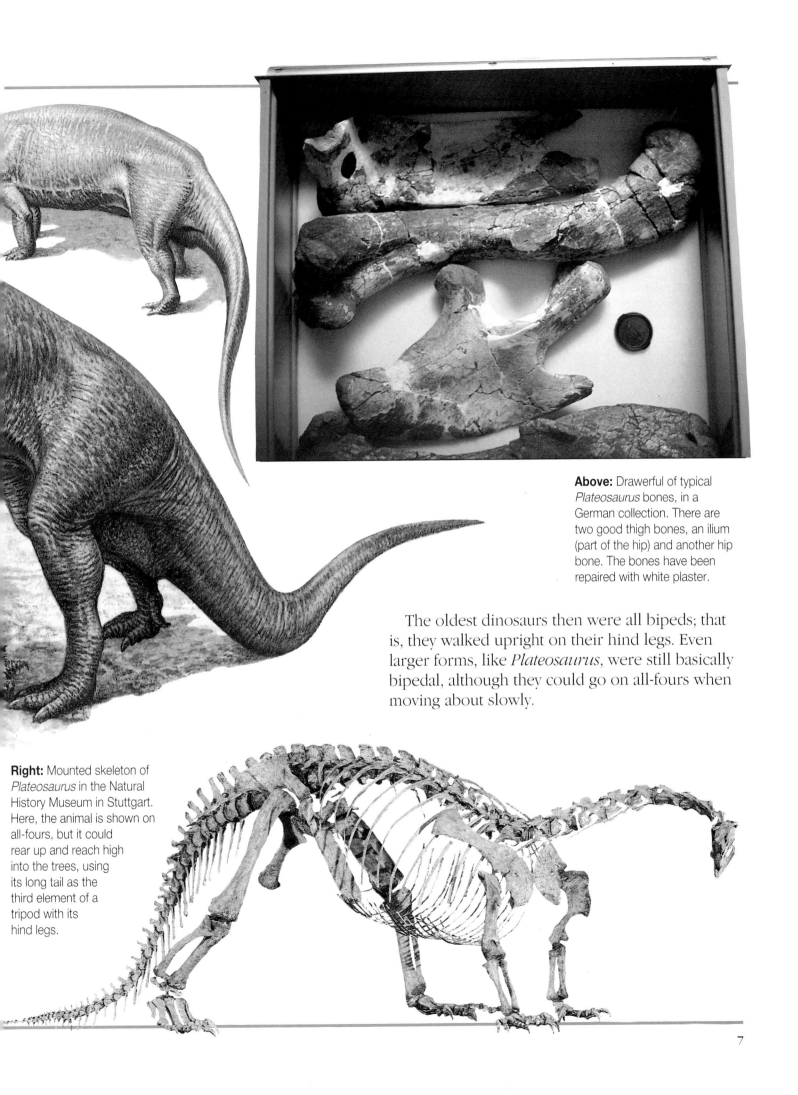

Above: Drawerful of typical *Plateosaurus* bones, in a German collection. There are two good thigh bones, an ilium (part of the hip) and another hip bone. The bones have been repaired with white plaster.

The oldest dinosaurs then were all bipeds; that is, they walked upright on their hind legs. Even larger forms, like *Plateosaurus*, were still basically bipedal, although they could go on all-fours when moving about slowly.

Right: Mounted skeleton of *Plateosaurus* in the Natural History Museum in Stuttgart. Here, the animal is shown on all-fours, but it could rear up and reach high into the trees, using its long tail as the third element of a tripod with its hind legs.

The First Dinosaurs

In North America, at about the time *Plateosaurus* and *Halticosaurus* were roaming in Germany, or perhaps a little earlier, the meat-eater *Coelophysis* seems to have been widespread. Its remains have been found in New Mexico, Arizona, and possibly also the Connecticut Valley. The first remains of this lightweight dinosaur were uncovered in 1881 and, although the bones were scrappy – a few vertebrae (the bony segments making up the backbone), rib fragments, hip bones and limb bones – the famous fossil hunter Edward Cope was able to name *three* species of *Coelophysis* from them!

This unsatisfactory state of affairs remained until 1947, when a field party from the American Museum of Natural History revisited the original locality, now on the land belonging to Ghost Ranch. The collectors found many bones of *Coelophysis*, all of which were in a single level of the rock formation. This layer was excavated that year, and the year after, by removing many tons of overburden from above. As the covering sediment was removed, dozens of complete skeletons of *Coelophysis* were exposed. The skeletons lay over one another in a tangled mass. It seems that a herd of these animals was caught in a flash flood produced by a sudden downpour and their bodies were washed along in the river and dumped on a sandbar.

Above: Edward Drinker Cope (1840-97), who named *Coelophysis*, among others!

There were small and large animals present, and it became clear that Cope's three supposed species were really all variations of one species: males and females, and young.

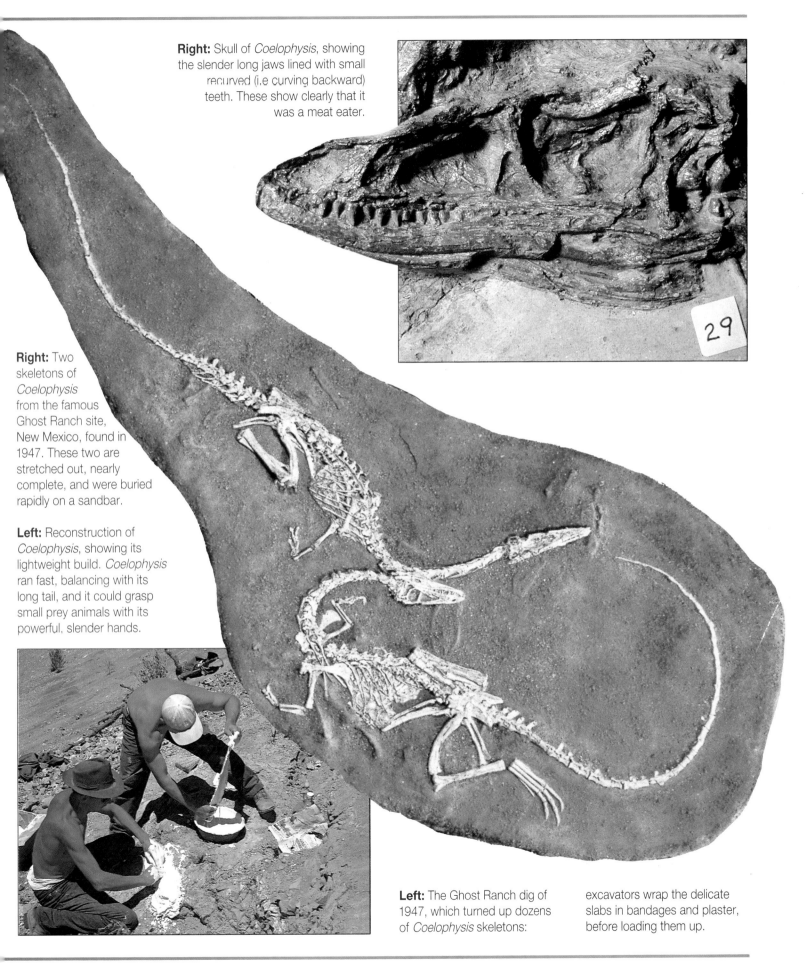

Right: Skull of *Coelophysis*, showing the slender long jaws lined with small recurved (i.e curving backward) teeth. These show clearly that it was a meat eater.

Right: Two skeletons of *Coelophysis* from the famous Ghost Ranch site, New Mexico, found in 1947. These two are stretched out, nearly complete, and were buried rapidly on a sandbar.

Left: Reconstruction of *Coelophysis*, showing its lightweight build. *Coelophysis* ran fast, balancing with its long tail, and it could grasp small prey animals with its powerful, slender hands.

Left: The Ghost Ranch dig of 1947, which turned up dozens of *Coelophysis* skeletons: excavators wrap the delicate slabs in bandages and plaster, before loading them up.

The Origin of the Dinosaurs

Where did these earliest dinosaurs come from? What were their closest relatives, and how did they come to take over the world during the Late Triassic?

The first point that has become clear from a great deal of recent study is that all the dinosaurs arose from a single ancestor. In other words, the great range of small and large meat-eaters, great lumbering plant-eaters and forms with armour and horns, can all be traced back to a single Late Triassic source. The Order Dinosauria is a real group, and it falls into two main subgroups, the Suborder Saurischia (the meat-eaters plus the large, long-necked plant-eaters) and the Suborder Ornithischia (all the rest). The two suborders are distinguished by the shape of their hip bones when seen in side view.

The dinosaurs were not the oldest animals known on the Earth. In fact they appeared quite

Above: Gideon Mantell (1790-1852). This English doctor was the discoverer of some of the first dinosaurs to be named, *Iguanodon* and *Hylaeosaurus*, in the 1820s.

Above: Skull and neck region of *Euparkeria*, which was quite a close ancestor of the dinosaurs. This small thecodontian lived in the Early Triassic in South Africa. It was a meat-eater.

Right: The huge skull of *Erythrosuchus*, an early thecodontian. This giant meat-eater, which was up to 4 metres (13ft) long, had huge jaws, and could have preyed on any plant-eater.

late in the day compared to the overall history of the Earth. The Earth is 4,600 million years old, and the dinosaurs arose 230 million years ago. To put things in perspective: if the entire history of the Earth was compressed into a single year, animals moved from the sea on to land about November, dinosaurs appeared on 12 December, and humans only on the evening of 31 December. For most of the early history of the Earth no life at all existed. When life did evolve, for a considerable time it manifested itself only as simple organic forms in the sea.

The dinosaurs are members of the larger group of reptiles called archosaurs (a term derived from the Greek meaning "ruling reptiles") which includes the crocodiles (the only surviving forms), the flying pterosaurs and, in the Triassic, the thecodontians, the ancestors of all the other groups.

The dinosaurs are an order of fossil reptiles, and they are divided into two suborders, the Saurischia and Ornithischia. Each of these suborders falls into several families of related animals, the Plateosauridae, Coelophysidae, Diplodocidae, and so on. These terms refer to particular ranks in the great scheme of classification of all living (and extinct) plants and animals.

The lowest rank is usually taken as the *species*, such as *Tyrannosaurus rex* or (in the case of man) *Homo sapiens*. Next up is the *genus* (plural, genera), such as *Tyrannosaurus* or *Homo*. Each genus may contain more than one species. The species and genera fall into families; modern examples are the Canidae (dogs, wolves, foxes), and the Equidae (horses, zebras, asses and so on). The families are then grouped in suborders and orders, and the orders into classes, phyla, and kingdoms. An outline of the position, and main divisions, of the dinosaurs is:

Kingdom Animalia (all animals)
  Phylum Chordata (all animals with backbones)
    Class Reptilia (turtles, lizards, snakes, crocodiles, etc.)
      Order Dinosauria
        Suborder Saurischia
          Infraorder Sauropodomorpha
            Family Thecodontosauridae
            Family Plateosauridae
            Family Cetiosauridae
            Family Camarasauridae
            Family Diplodocidae
            Family Brachiosauridae
            Family Titanosauridae
          Infraorder Theropoda
            Family Coelophysidae
            Family Megalosauridae
            Family Tyrannosauridae
            Family Coeluridae
            Family Ornithomimidae
            Family Oviraptoridae
            Family Deinonychidae
          Infraorder Segnosauria (?)
        Suborder Ornithischia
          Infraorder Thyreophora
            Family Scelidosauridae
            Family Nodosauridae
            Family Ankylosauridae
            Family Stegosauridae
          Infraorder Ornithopoda
            Family Fabrosauridae
            Family Heterodontosauridae
            Family Hypsilophodontidae
            Family Iguanodontidae
            Family Hadrosauridae
          Infraorder Marginocephalia
            Family Pachycephalosauridae
            Family Ceratopsidae

The three-pronged "lizard hip" of the meat-eating and giant plant-eating saurischians.

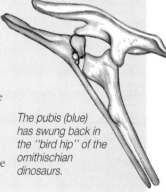

The pubis (blue) has swung back in the "bird hip" of the ornithischian dinosaurs.

Right: The skull of *Herrerasaurus*, the oldest-known dinosaur, from the Late Triassic of Argentina. It was a carnivore.

The First Plant-Eaters

Above: The pelvis of a large prosauropod dinosaur in the course of excavation in Lesotho, southern Africa. The hammer shows its size.

Left: The hindlimb of the prosauropod *Massospondylus* being dug out in southern Africa. The bones are exposed like this in the field, and are then packed for transport to the museum.

The plant-eating dinosaurs of the Late Triassic and the Early Jurassic, the time span from about 225 to 187 million years ago, were the prosauropods, animals like *Plateosaurus* (see pages 6-7 and 16-17). The first prosauropods were smaller than *Plateosaurus*, while some later examples achieved considerable sizes.

Thecodontosaurus from the Late Triassic of southern England and South Wales was actually one of the first dinosaurs to be discovered, in the 1830s. It was named in 1840 on the basis of a piece of jawbone found within the city of Bristol. Since then many other bones and partial skeletons have been discovered, which have allowed a restoration of its appearance in life. The odd thing about

Above: *Massospondylus* is attacked by a pack of meat-eating *Syntarsus*. This small relative of *Coelophysis* may have been able to tackle larger prey if it hunted in packs.

Left: Skeleton of *Massospondylus* in the South African Museum, Cape Town, showing how high it could rear up on its hind legs in order to forage for food in the trees.

Thecodontosaurus is where these bones have been found. They have all come from ancient fissures, or open cave systems, which were formed in older limestones during the Triassic. Small animals, including *Thecodontosaurus*, apparently fell down these fissures, and became trapped. The fissures can now be excavated, and they supply unique insights into the smaller, more delicate animals that are often not preserved in rougher river conditions.

Later prosauropods, such as *Riojasaurus* from Argentina, reached very large size: 11 metres (36ft) long in this case, and by Early Jurassic times, many forms, such as *Vulcanodon* from Zimbabwe, were on the borderline of becoming true sauropods, the giants of the Jurassic and Cretaceous (see pages 24-27).

Left: Another view of the *Massospondylus* excavation, showing parts of the backbone and hindlimb as they lay in the ground. The skeleton is remarkably complete, and only minimally disturbed by water movement after the animal died.

Deep Time and Moving Continents

Geologists are scientists who study the history of the Earth as revealed in its changing rock forms. They deal in almost unimaginably long spans of time. The evidence for geological ages has to be obtained from the rocks and fossils that are found in a succession of layers (known as strata) that are exposed at the surface of the Earth. In the early nineteenth century, geologists noticed that the deepest rocks (the oldest ones) contained the fossils of very simple plants and animals. On moving up, fishes and land plants were found, then amphibians, then reptiles, then mammals and birds. These early geologists also realised that there were particular groups of fossils that were always found together, and that seemed to be typical of particular rock formations. These two principles – progress in the history of life, and repeated fossil associations – allowed the early geologists to categorise the rocks of the Earth in a particular order according to their relative age, and to identify rock units of similar age by the fossils they contain, even if they were found in different parts of the world.

Having got the rocks roughly into order, geologists began to work on ways of determining their exact dates in millions of years. This is done by looking at rates of natural radioactive decay of a variety of elements which can be measured by scientific instruments: the older the rock, the more decay will have taken place.

Geological time scales are hard to comprehend; the fact that the surface of the Earth is actually made up of many large, rocky plates that are in constant motion seems an even more bizarre concept. Nevertheless, this is the case and the rates of movement can be measured, and felt in the form of earthquakes. During Triassic times, all continents were fused together as one, and dinosaurs could roam freely all over the world. For example, the North American prosauropod *Anchisaurus* has also been found in South Africa. After the Triassic, however, new seaways formed, the Atlantic and Indian Oceans opened up, and the continents moved slowly but surely towards the positions they now occupy.

Above: Working in the dinosaur-bearing rocks in the badlands of Alberta, Canada. Note the layering of the rocks.

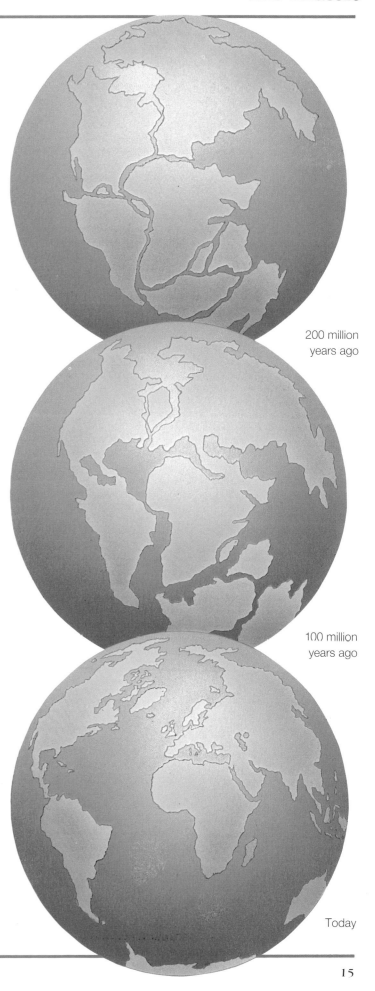

Above: Excavation of a duckbilled dinosaur, showing the backbone in the middle, ribs above, and the tail below.

Below: The badlands of the South Saskatchewan River in Alberta, Canada. The sudden rains wash away layers of soft sediments, leaving the ancient layered rocks bare of plant cover. These are ''good lands'' for dinosaur prospecting.

Right: The changing face of the Earth over the last 200 million years. When the dinosaurs arose, in the Triassic, all continents were fused to form a single great land mass. The North Atlantic opened up in the Jurassic, and the South Atlantic in the Cretaceous. Southern continents were also on the move, and by 100 million years ago the layout of the world was more like it is today.

200 million years ago

100 million years ago

Today

Herds of Dinosaurs

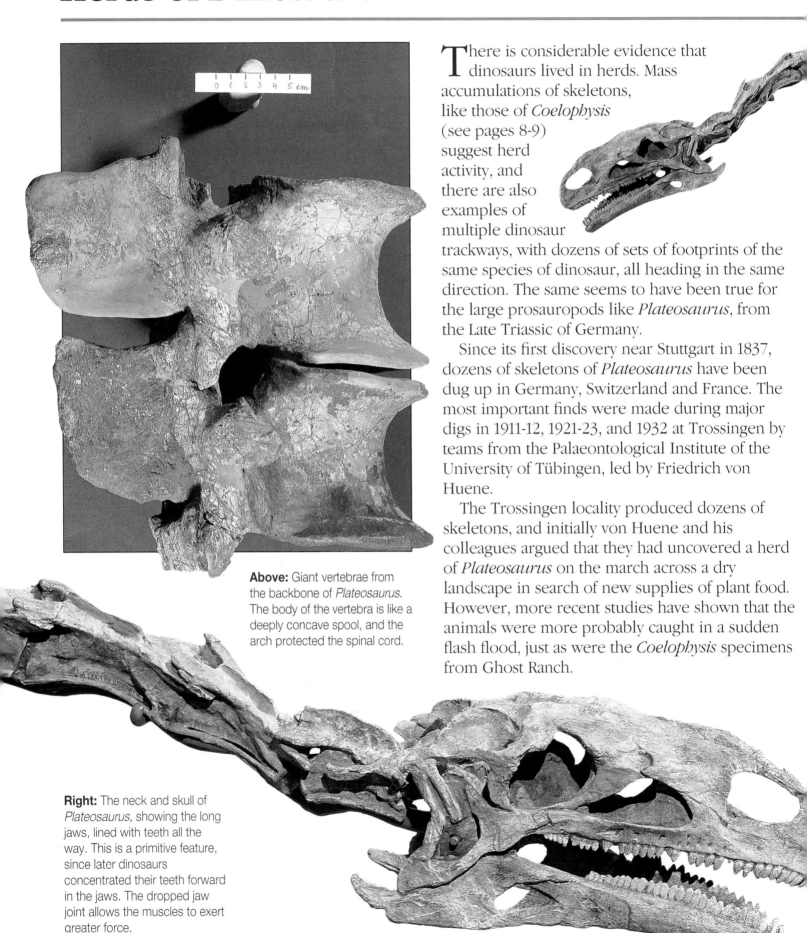

There is considerable evidence that dinosaurs lived in herds. Mass accumulations of skeletons, like those of *Coelophysis* (see pages 8-9) suggest herd activity, and there are also examples of multiple dinosaur trackways, with dozens of sets of footprints of the same species of dinosaur, all heading in the same direction. The same seems to have been true for the large prosauropods like *Plateosaurus*, from the Late Triassic of Germany.

Since its first discovery near Stuttgart in 1837, dozens of skeletons of *Plateosaurus* have been dug up in Germany, Switzerland and France. The most important finds were made during major digs in 1911-12, 1921-23, and 1932 at Trossingen by teams from the Palaeontological Institute of the University of Tübingen, led by Friedrich von Huene.

The Trossingen locality produced dozens of skeletons, and initially von Huene and his colleagues argued that they had uncovered a herd of *Plateosaurus* on the march across a dry landscape in search of new supplies of plant food. However, more recent studies have shown that the animals were more probably caught in a sudden flash flood, just as were the *Coelophysis* specimens from Ghost Ranch.

Above: Giant vertebrae from the backbone of *Plateosaurus*. The body of the vertebra is like a deeply concave spool, and the arch protected the spinal cord.

Right: The neck and skull of *Plateosaurus*, showing the long jaws, lined with teeth all the way. This is a primitive feature, since later dinosaurs concentrated their teeth forward in the jaws. The dropped jaw joint allows the muscles to exert greater force.

Left: Skeleton of *Plateosaurus* mounted in the Stuttgart Natural History Museum. The long neck was used to allow the animal to reach high into food-bearing trees. Vast herds of these animals were buried by flash floods.

Right: Friedrich von Huene (1875-1970), the great expert on *Plateosaurus*.

Below: Excavation of the Ghost Ranch *Coelophysis* specimens. Like many finds of *Plateosaurus*, these had been preserved during a flash flood.

3 The Jurassic

The dinosaurs of the Early Jurassic were mainly like those of the Late Triassic; prosauropods (see pages 12-13) and meat-eaters like *Coelophysis* (see pages 8-9), with a few new plant-eating types (see pages 20-21). Major new groups came on the scene during the Middle and Late Jurassic: large meat-eaters (see pages 22-23), the giant plant-eating sauropods (see pages 24-27), the stegosaurs (see pages 28-29), the bipedal plant-eaters (see pages 30-31), and new small meat-eaters (see pages 32-33).

The Late Jurassic rocks of the Morrison Formation of Utah and Colorado contain some of the best-known "classic" dinosaurs: *Allosaurus*, *Apatosaurus* (= *Brontosaurus*), *Diplodocus*, *Stegosaurus* and others. These were all first collected in the heroic days of American palaeontology, between 1870 and 1900, by teams sent out by the arch-rivals Edward Cope and Othniel Marsh. The collectors extracted the huge bones at great speed, and often in awful conditions, and sent them east by the trainload. Between them, Cope and Marsh named 130 new species of dinosaurs from the American Midwest.

Jurassic climates were still warm, as in the Triassic, but probably not so dry. The Morrison

Above: Othniel Charles Marsh (1831-99), the great dinosaur hunter and rival of Cope.

Right: The meat-eater *Allosaurus* stalks its prey while carcasses and skeletons lying on the river bank are on their way to becoming fossils.

landscape was covered with tall conifer trees, and a variety of low waterside plants on the sides of broad meandering rivers. Climates were seasonal, with cooler winters, but no snow.

Right: This motley crew of dinosaur hunters, led by Othniel Marsh (centre back), were operating in the American Western Territories in 1872. Note the guns and knives!

Left: A technician prepares giant dinosaur bones out of the rock at Dinosaur National Monument in Colorado. Here, during the Jurassic, hundreds of skeletons were washed together and dumped on a sandbar.

Above: Vast thicknesses of Jurassic sediments, containing dinosaur bones, are exposed in the area of Dinosaur National Monument, in Utah and in Colorado.

The First Armoured Dinosaurs

Three dinosaurs, one from southern England, one from the southwestern U.S., and one from southern Africa, document the first occurrence of armour of different forms in the Early Jurassic. The English dinosaur, *Scelidosaurus*, was named in 1860 from a collection of odd bones and a nearly complete skeleton found in the marine sediments of Dorset. Some new specimens have come to light recently, and these have allowed detailed studies to be undertaken. *Scelidosaurus* was a 4 metre- (13ft-) long animal, and it probably walked most of the time on all-fours. It was a plant-eater, as revealed by its teeth, and it had broad hoof-like toe nails. The armour consisted of numerous oval-shaped bony plates, each 5-10cm (2-4in) long, lying in long rows over the neck, the back, the sides and the tail. These bony plates were fixed firmly into the skin, and they presumably served to protect the animal from attacks by meat-eaters.

The early American armoured dinosaur is *Scutellosaurus*, named only in 1981, but obviously a close relative of *Scelidosaurus*. It was nearly twice as long, and may still have been largely bipedal. However, the armour was similar to that

Above: Skeleton of the early ornithischian dinosaur *Heterodontosaurus* from the Early Jurassic of South Africa. This small biped had different forms of teeth, with tusks for use in fighting.

Left: The Lesotho Red Beds which have produced many of the best skeletons of early dinosaurs, especially *Heterodontosaurus*. The extensive exposure allows dinosaur hunters to scour the ground for bones at all times.

Right: Excavation of a small dinosaur skeleton in the Red Beds of Lesotho. Here, the South African palaeontologists A. W. Crompton and R. F. Ewer are at work.

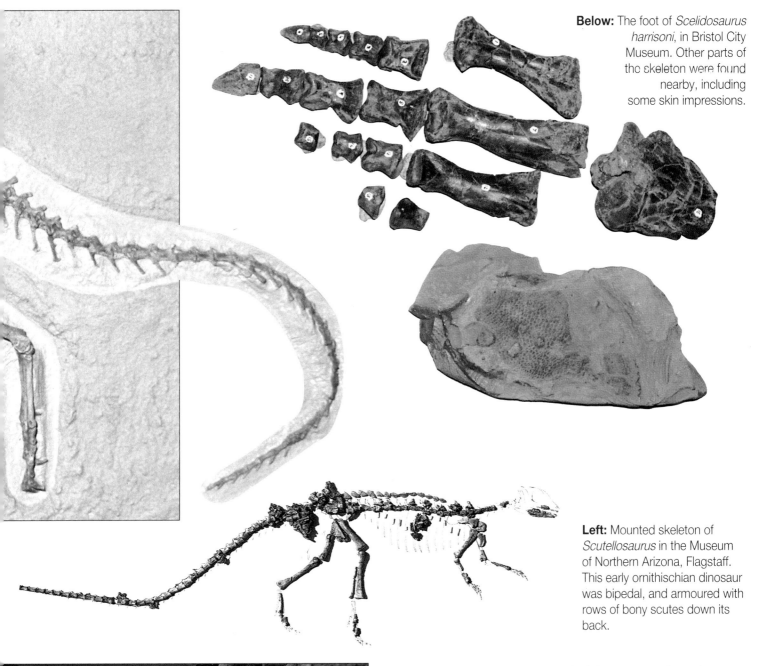

Below: The foot of *Scelidosaurus harrisoni*, in Bristol City Museum. Other parts of the skeleton were found nearby, including some skin impressions.

Left: Mounted skeleton of *Scutellosaurus* in the Museum of Northern Arizona, Flagstaff. This early ornithischian dinosaur was bipedal, and armoured with rows of bony scutes down its back.

of *Scelidosaurus*, and probably ancestral to the later stegosaurs (see pages 28-29) and ankylosaurs (see pages 54-55).

The early South African armoured dinosaur is rather different. This is *Heterodontosaurus*, a small plant-eater, only 1.2 metres (4ft) long, named in 1962. *Heterodontosaurus* did not have any body armour, but it did have very unusual teeth. In particular, many specimens (perhaps they are males?) have sharp, tusk-like side teeth, which may have been used in defence, just as pigs can defend themselves with their sharp fangs.

The Big Meat-Eaters

Large meat-eating dinosaurs first appeared in the Middle Jurassic. For the first 40 million years of dinosaur evolution, there were no meat-eating dinosaurs large enough to kill and eat other dinosaurs. One of the first of these new and fearsome predators was *Megalosaurus* from the Middle Jurassic of Europe.

The first bone of *Megalosaurus* had actually been found in 1677, but it was thought to be a bone from a giant human! More bones came to light over the years in the limestone quarries north of Oxford, England, and one of these was a jaw bone bearing several large teeth with serrated zig-zag edges, just like steak knives. Dean William Buckland, Professor of Geology at Oxford University, realised that the bones all came from some kind of giant reptile,

Right: The first dinosaur ever to be named, *Megalosaurus* from the Middle Jurassic of England. This animal may have been ancestral to later giant carnivores.

Below: Skull of the meat-eater *Allosaurus*, showing the knife-like teeth, and the light construction of the skull. Where bone could be saved, it was lost, in order to make the head lighter. Strength was not sacrificed, since thick girders of bone remained.

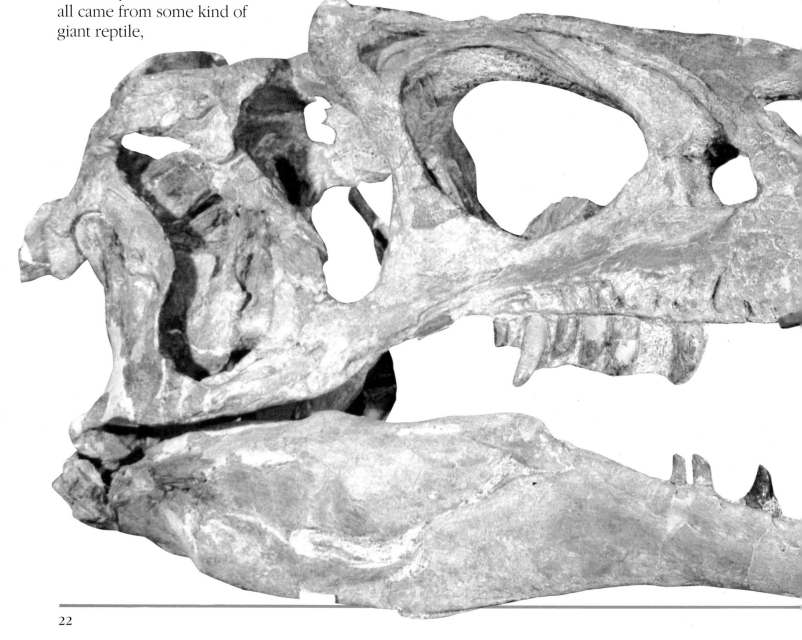

and in 1824 he named it *Megalosaurus*, which means "big reptile" in Greek. This was the first dinosaur ever to be named.

In the Late Jurassic, the meat-eaters grew even larger and more diverse. In the Morrison Formation of Utah and Colorado, for example, there were two well-known forms, *Allosaurus* and *Ceratosaurus*. The first of these was 12 metres (39ft) long, and the second was 6 metres (19.5ft) long. Both would clearly have been able to attack and consume many of the dinosaurs around at that time. Even the large sauropods (see pages 24-27) were not completely immune from attack. *Allosaurus* was probably large enough, and fast enough, to attack at least juveniles and older weaker animals that were much larger than itself.

Left: Model of *Allosaurus*, showing its running style. The long tail is held out straight behind as a balancing rod at high speeds.

Below: A technician prepares a fine specimen of the skull of *Allosaurus*. This is preserved nearly uncrushed in the Late Jurassic rocks of Colorado.

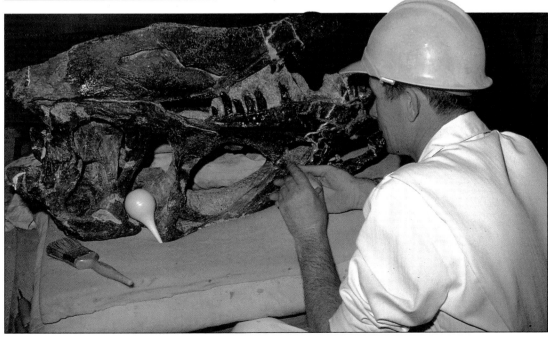

The Giant Plant-Eaters

Left: The heavily-built sauropod *Camarasaurus* browsing on vegetation in Late Jurassic times in the American Midwest. The long neck allowed *Camarasaurus* to feed high in the trees, mainly conifers, that grew in lowland areas.

Below: The short-snouted skull of *Camarasaurus* shows how the numbers of teeth have declined when compared with the earlier *Plateosaurus*. The openings in the skull are for the nostrils, eye sockets, and jaw muscle attachments.

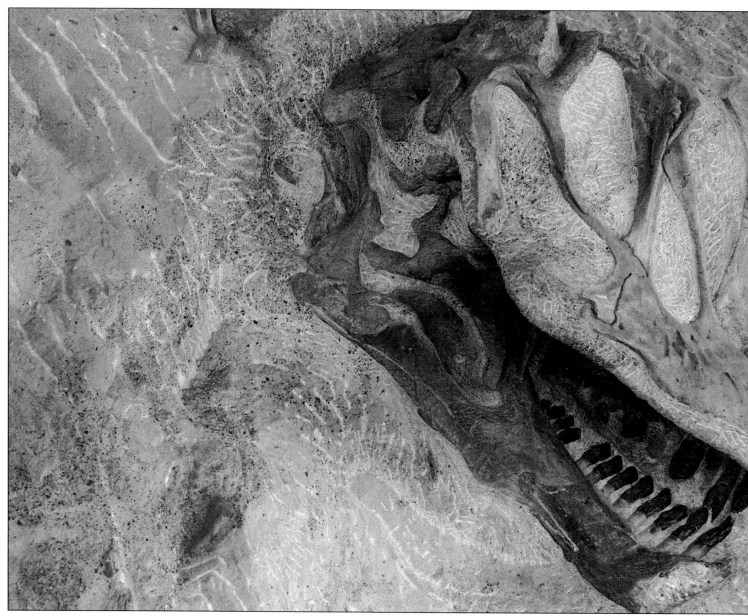

The giant plant-eating dinosaurs are known as the sauropods. They evolved from the prosauropods during the Early Jurassic, and animals like *Vulcanodon* are close to the borderline between the two. An early true sauropod was *Barapasaurus* from India, which is known from hundreds of bones found scattered over a wide area. The teeth of meat-eating dinosaurs were found among these large bones; this suggests that they were feeding on the carcasses.

During the 1830s, several enormous vertebrae came to light in different parts of England. Some of the best were found with *Megalosaurus* fossils. At first these bones were thought to come from the backbones of whales. The English scientist Richard Owen thought the bones were those of a giant sea-crocodile, and consequently he named it *Cetiosaurus* ("whale reptile") in 1841. It was only in 1869, when much more of the skeleton came to light, that it was identified as a dinosaur. The cetiosaurids were important Middle Jurassic sauropods, up to 18 metres (59ft) long. Close relatives, such as *Shunosaurus* and *Datousaurus* lived at the same time in China.

The real flowering of the sauropods happened in the Late Jurassic, when the camarasaurids, brachiosaurids and diplodocids arose (see also pages 26-27). *Camarasaurus* from Colorado was 18 metres (59ft) long, and rather heavily built. Its skull was short and high, and the teeth rather chisel-like. Although huge, as we shall see, the camarasaurids were not the largest of the sauropods.

Above: Richard Owen (1804-92), with the fossil bird *Dinornis*.

Above: Vertebrae of the early sauropod *Cetiosaurus* from the Middle Jurassic of England, a form named by Richard Owen.

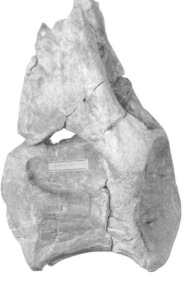

Right: Digging up the leg bone of an early sauropod, *Barapasaurus*, from the Early Jurassic of India.

Even Larger Plant-Eaters

The brachiosaurids and diplodocids are probably the best-known sauropods. *Brachiosaurus* was first reported from Colorado in 1900 on the basis of a rather incomplete skeleton. Further information about this dinosaur came from Africa soon after. In 1907, a German prospector chanced upon a rich dinosaur deposit at Tendaguru in Tanzania (then German East Africa). A series of massive expeditions was set up from 1908-1912, during which time over 250 tonnes (246 tons) of fossil bones were carried to the coast, and shipped out to Berlin, Germany. One of the most impressive specimens was a complete skeleton of *Brachiosaurus*.

This showed that its total length was 22.5 metres (74.5ft), and that *Brachiosaurus* could raise its head to the amazing height of 12 metres (39ft), that is, the height of a four-storey building. Like a giraffe, *Brachiosaurus* had a long neck with powerful muscles to lift it to a vertical position, and its forelimbs were longer than its hindlimbs, to give it extra height. It may seem unusual that the same kind of dinosaur was found in North America and in Africa. However, recall that at this time, all the continents were joined together, and the large sauropods could wander freely across the globe.

The diplodocids, like *Diplodocus* (27 metres, 88.5ft long) and *Apatosaurus* (21 metres, 69ft long) were more lightly built, and equipped with long, whip-like tails. They had long skulls and reduced peg-like teeth. Since 1970 some even larger

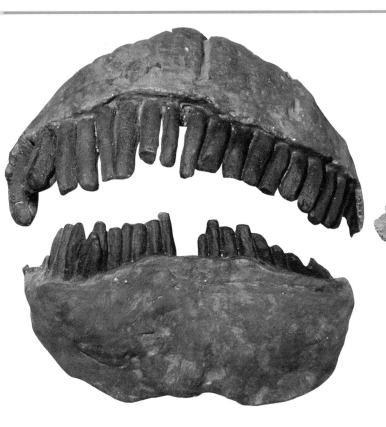

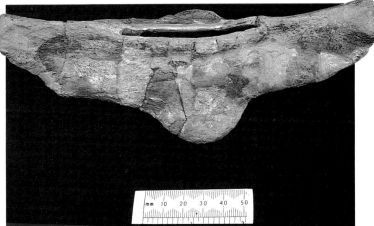

sauropods have been reported from the Late Triassic of North America: *Supersaurus* (25-30 metres, 82-98ft long?), *Ultrasaurus* (30 metres, 98ft long?), and "*Seismosaurus*" (35-40 metres, 115-131ft long?). Unfortunately, none of these sauropods is completely known, and so the lengths are largely guesswork.

Above: The front of the jaws of *Diplodocus*, showing the numerous cylindrical peg-like teeth crowded closely together, and rooted deeply in the jaw bones. These were used for tearing up large quantities of plant food for swallowing.

Left: Skeleton of the longest complete dinosaur known, *Diplodocus carnegii*, one of several casts sent out by the Carnegie Museum, Pittsburgh, Pennsylvania. Its size can be assessed by comparison with *Iguanodon bernissartensis*, a plant-eater to its right.

Right: Reconstruction of the largest discovered dinosaurs. *Brachiosaurus* (middle) is known from nearly complete skeletons from Tanzania and from the western United States. The other two, *Ultrasaurus* (left) and *Supersaurus* (right), are based on partial remains, which were very large, but their exact size is hard to estimate.

Above: The strange boat-like "chevron" bone of *Diplodocus*, the reason for its name, which means "double beam". The chevron bones lie below the vertebrae of the tail.

The Plated Dinosaurs

The stegosaurs were another remarkable new dinosaur group of the Middle and Late Jurassic. The oldest ones are found with *Megalosaurus* and *Cetiosaurus* in the Middle Jurassic of southern England. The early English forms, *Dacentrurus* and *Lexovisaurus* had rows of spines and narrow plates down the middle of their backs. The same is true of the Middle Jurassic stegosaurs from China, *Huayangosaurus* and *Tuojiangosaurus*, found in the 1970s.

The Late Jurassic stegosaurs are rather better known. Different forms lived in Tanzania in Africa and in North America, although some of the sauropod dinosaurs in both areas were the same (see pages 26-27). The Tanzanian *Kentrosaurus* was relatively small, only 2.5 metres (8.2ft) long, and it bore narrow plates on its back and spines on its tail. The North American *Stegosaurus* was 6 to 7 metres (20-25ft) long, and it developed broad, lozenge-shaped plates on its back, and spines only at the end of its tail.

It has usually been assumed that the plates and spines protected stegosaurs from attack by the large meat-eaters of their day. This may have been partly true, but the plates did not actually cover the vulnerable sides of the body. It may be that they also had a function in temperature control. The plates were covered with skin in life, and they contained many blood vessels. In hot weather, blood would be pumped to the plates, and excess heat radiated into the atmosphere. On colder days, the blood vessels to the plates may have been shut down, and body heat conserved.

Above: Skull of one of the first stegosaurs, *Huayangosaurus taibaii*, from the Middle Jurassic of China. The snout is long, and is lined with small diamond-shaped teeth.

Below: Reconstruction of the Late Jurassic stegosaur *Kentrosaurus* from Tanzania, by Greg Paul. Note the long spines, and shorter plates just behind the head.

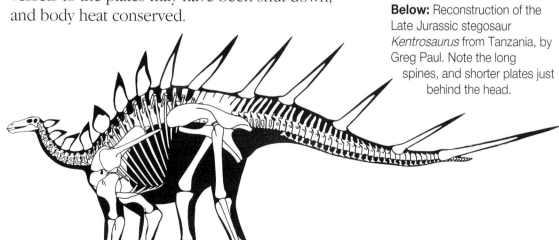

Left: Excavation of the tiny bones of a juvenile *Stegosaurus* found in Late Jurassic sediments at Dinosaur National Monument, Colorado, in the 1970s. It was probably only a year old when it died.

Right: A stegosaur gallery: *Stegosaurus* (top), *Tuojiangosaurus* (top right), *Kentrosaurus* (bottom right), *Lexovisaurus* (middle), and *Dacentrurus* (bottom left)

Below: The best-known stegosaur, *Stegosaurus*: a mounted skeleton and painting. The plates on the back are shown in a double row, but this layout is not certain, and they may have stood in a single row.

Stegosaurus

Stegosaurus had a narrow body and a heavy, spiked tail. Its back legs were almost twice as long as its front legs. This planteater may have reared on its hind legs to reach tall vegetation.

Stegosaurus armatus

The New Plant-Eaters

Other new groups of plant-eaters developed in the Late Jurassic. As we have seen, the ornithopods, unarmoured bipedal ornithischian dinosaurs, had arisen in the Late Triassic or Early Jurassic. New forms appeared in the Late Jurassic, and these were heralds of what was to come soon after (see pages 36-37, 40-41).

Dryosaurus from North America and Tanzania in Africa was 3 to 4 metres (10-13ft) long, and it was an agile and active biped. Its head was short, and the teeth were highly specialised for chopping up tough plants. The sauropods of the same time had peg-like teeth that could only really have dealt with soft leaves, and it may be that the smaller ornithopods succeeded them because of their more advanced eating equipment. *Dryosaurus* had short arms and long legs for rapid running. Its tail was held out straight behind as a kind of balancing rod to stabilise it at high speed. *Dryosaurus* seems to have established itself worldwide, just like some of the other Tendaguru animals.

Camptosaurus was a close relative, a 5 to 7 metre- (16-23ft-) long ornithopod. It is also known from a number of parts of the world: North America and Europe. The skull of *Camptosaurus* is long and almost horse-like in shape. The tips of the snout and lower jaw bear no teeth at all, only a sharp beak made of bone. Behind this lies a series of broad teeth that were capable of a primitive kind of chewing action.

Below: Internal view of the right upper jaws of *Camptosaurus* from the Late Jurassic of England. The ridged teeth formed a grinding surface for dealing with tough plants.

Right: Reconstructed scene with the large theropod *Allosaurus* attacking the plant-eating ornithopod *Camptosaurus*, based on skeletons from the Late Jurassic of North America.

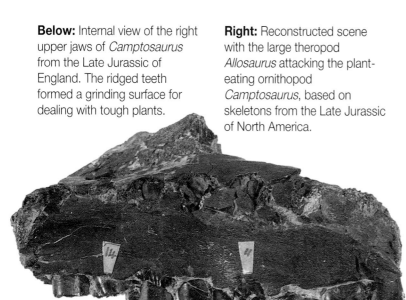

Left: Vertebrae of the large ornithopod *Camptosaurus* from the Late Jurassic of England. The smallest ones come from the end of the tail, the larger ones from the back.

Above: Skull of the ornithopod *Dryosaurus altus*, the North American species, which had a very close relative in Africa. Plants were broken up with the broad cheek teeth in the middle and back parts of the jaws.

Below: The skeleton of *Camptosaurus browni* from the Late Jurassic of North America. This large ornithopod walked on all-tours or on its hindlimbs alone, especially when it was running fast.

Above: Skull of *Dryosaurus*, showing the powerful teeth and the shortened face. The skull was in many ways the same shape as a sheep's

Small Meat-Eaters and Birds

The sedimentary deposits of a remarkable ancient lagoon at Solnhofen in southern Germany have preserved some of the most exquisite fossils of small dinosaurs, as well as numerous other animals. The detail is so fantastic that not only are tiny bones seen complete in every detail, but also the soft body outlines of fishes and lizards, and even completely soft-bodied animals like worms and jellyfishes are preserved. The deposits of this lagoon have turned into a very fine limestone that was quarried last century to make engraved printing plates, and it is still quarried today for its fossils.

In the late 1850s a remarkable little skeleton came to light at Solnhofen. This was a 1 metre-(3ft-) long, bipedal, meat-eating dinosaur named *Compsognathus*. Its head was lightweight, had a very large eye socket, and rows of tiny, needle-sharp teeth. The legs were thin and the tail extremely long. Inside the rib cage was the skeleton of a large lizard, obviously the last meal of this small dinosaur.

Another small lightweight skeleton was found at Solnhofen in 1861. In nearly all respects, the bones

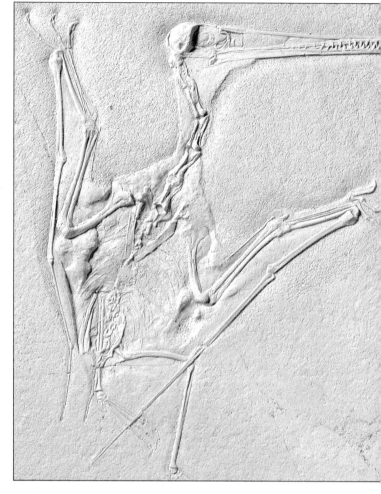

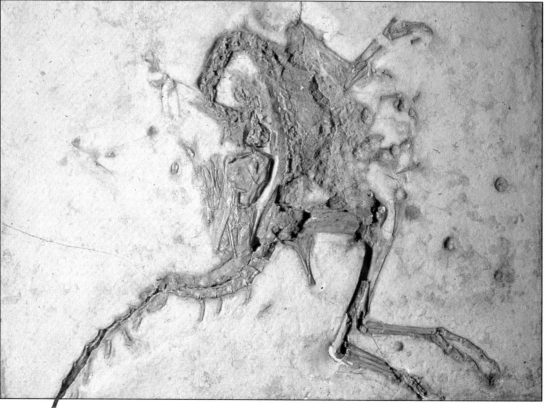

Above: *Pterodactylus kochi*, a pigeon-sized pterosaur beautifully preserved in the mudstones of Solnhofen in Germany. Traces of the skin around its throat and in the wings can even be seen.

Left: The beautiful skeleton of *Compsognathus longipes* in the Bavarian State Geological Museum in Munich. This is the smallest known adult dinosaur. Inside the rib cage are the remains of its last meal, a lizard called *Bavarisaurus*.

Right: The rarest fossil of all, a complete specimen of *Archaeopteryx*, in the Humboldt Museum, Berlin. The body is stretched out, with the head bent back because of drying out of the carcass, and the wing and tail feathers are clear.

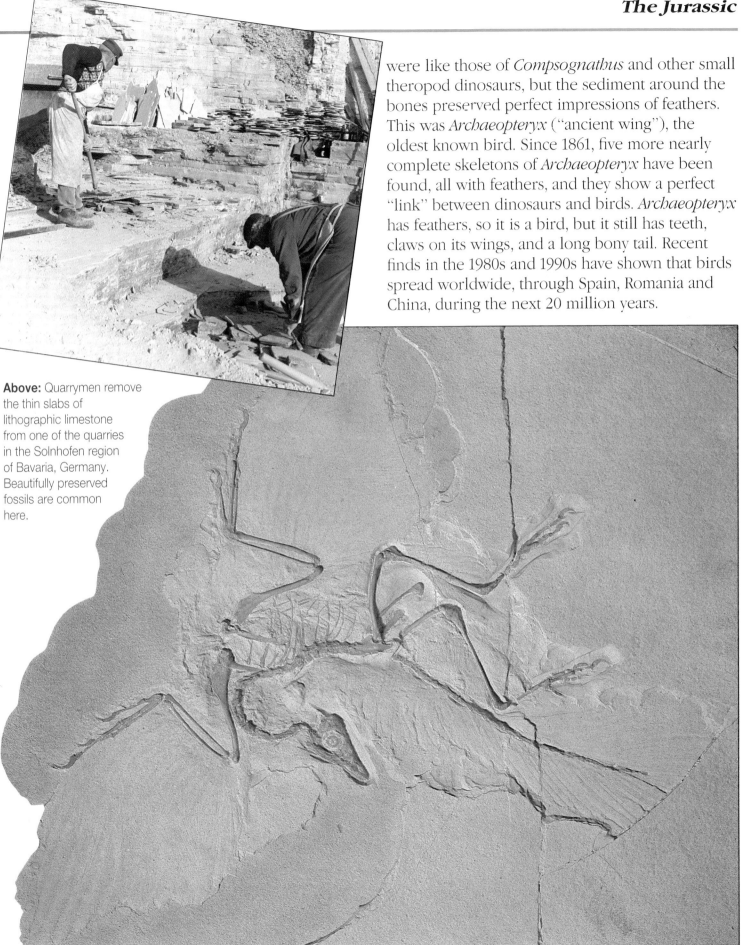

were like those of *Compsognathus* and other small theropod dinosaurs, but the sediment around the bones preserved perfect impressions of feathers. This was *Archaeopteryx* ("ancient wing"), the oldest known bird. Since 1861, five more nearly complete skeletons of *Archaeopteryx* have been found, all with feathers, and they show a perfect "link" between dinosaurs and birds. *Archaeopteryx* has feathers, so it is a bird, but it still has teeth, claws on its wings, and a long bony tail. Recent finds in the 1980s and 1990s have shown that birds spread worldwide, through Spain, Romania and China, during the next 20 million years.

Above: Quarrymen remove the thin slabs of lithographic limestone from one of the quarries in the Solnhofen region of Bavaria, Germany. Beautifully preserved fossils are common here.

The Early Cretaceous World

Dinosaurs evolved into several major new groups in the Early Cretaceous, the time from 144 to 98 million years ago. The best-known dinosaurs of this age come from southern England and parts of central Europe, and from Montana in the United States.

The English Wealden has been recognised as a rich source of dinosaurs since the 1820s. Indeed, the second dinosaur ever to be named was *Iguanodon*, which was found in Wealden deposits in 1825 (see pages 40-41). The iguanodontids and the hypsilophodontids were the dominant plant-eaters at this time. Derived from ornithopods like *Camptosaurus* from the Late Jurassic, these new forms had highly efficient jaw systems, and they probably browsed on low bushes and trees in huge herds. The giant sauropods were still present, but by now very rare; a big change from the Late Jurassic scene.

New kinds of armoured plant-eating dinosaurs came on the scene in the Early Cretaceous (see pages 42-43), and these were preyed upon by new meat-eaters, many of them armed with vicious slashing claws (see pages 38-39).

Below: An excavation in the Wealden (Early Cretaceous) of the Isle of Wight, England. Abundant dinosaur skeletons come to light every year after storms which wash off soft sediments along the coast.

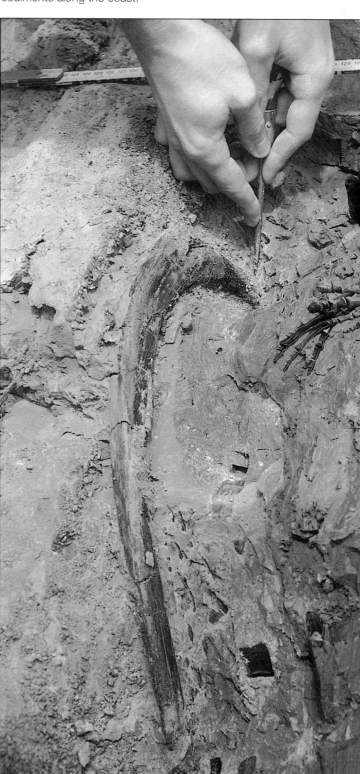

Above: Skeleton of *Iguanodon* in the course of excavation from Early Cretaceous rock strata in the Isle of Wight.

Above: Microscopic thin section of dinosaur bone from the Early Cretaceous Wealden of the Isle of Wight. Pore spaces in the original bone are filled with minerals.

The Early Cretaceous world showed some signs of continental break-up, with rather different dinosaurs being found in different parts of the world. Climates in Europe and North America were warm and seasonal. Many of the dinosaur fossils have been found close to rivers in broad delta plains. Associated animals included frogs, salamanders, turtles, crocodilians, lizards, the earliest snakes, flying pterosaurs (often quite large ones), early birds and mammals.

Above: Skeleton of *Iguanodon atherfieldensis*, the typical Wealden dinosaur, known from southern England, Belgium and Germany. Note the great thumb claw, possibly used in defence.

The Flowering of the Ornithopods

The first really successful ornithischians (see pages 10-11 for an explanation of this term) were the hypsilophodontids. They arose first in the Late Jurassic, with forms like *Dryosaurus* achieving worldwide distribution. In the Early Cretaceous, the hypsilophodontids radiated even more widely, being known from North America, Europe, South America, Australia and Antarctica.

The best-known hypsilophodontid is *Hypsilophodon* itself from the Wealden deposits of the Isle of Wight, southern England. The first skeletons were found in 1849, but interpreted then as juvenile specimens of *Iguanodon* (see pages 40-41). Later, when more complete skeletons came to light, this was recognised as a distinctive animal. Skeletons are still turning up today, and indeed one level of rocks on the Isle of Wight is known as the "*Hypsilophodon* Bed" because so many have been found there.

Hypsilophodon has a short skull, no teeth at the front of the jaws, and a long row of cheek teeth further back. Like a sheep, *Hypsilophodon* must have nipped off leaves with the toothless front part of its snout, moved them back with its tongue and "chewed" them in a way that was unique to ornithopods. *Hypsilophodon*, *Iguanodon* and their relatives could flex the cheek regions of their skulls in and out. There was an extra joint between the bones along the side of the face, and as the jaws closed around a mouthful of leaves, the upper jaws splayed outwards. When the lower jaw

moved down, the upper jaws moved back inwards. This remarkable in-and-out chewing technique may have given these advanced ornithopods the edge over other plant-eating dinosaurs which could not chew their food. Like all other reptiles, most dinosaurs could simply open and shut their mouths like the hinge of a door, and food had to be swallowed unchewed.

The Early Cretaceous

Right: Excavation of a skeleton of *Hypsilophodon* on the Isle of Wight. It seems that this modest-sized ornithopod was immensely common, and it probably browsed on low bushes in large herds.

Right: Reconstruction of *Hypsilophodon foxi*, based on numerous skeletons. At one time it was thought that *Hypsilophodon* perched in trees, but the strong feet could not grasp branches, and are clearly designed for fast running.

Below: Skull of one of the last hypsilophodontids, *Parksosaurus warreni*, from Alberta, Canada. The short jaws bear ridged teeth in the cheek region, used for cutting up plant food. There were no teeth at the front, merely a bony plate.

Above: A palaeontologist points to the "*Hypsilophodon* Bed" in the Wealden of the Isle of Wight, southern England. This is the source of numerous fine skeletons of the small ornithopod *Hypsilophodon*.

Left: Skeleton of *Thescelosaurus* from the Late Cretaceous of North America, a later relative of *Hypsilophodon*. When running, the tail was held out straight behind as a balancing rod, since the centre of gravity lay over the hip.

The Sickle Claws

It is often mistakenly thought that all the most exciting dinosaurs were found years ago. Especially in North America and Europe, where people have been collecting for years, surely there is nothing new? Dramatic discoveries of the last decades have proved this wrong. Two new dinosaurs unearthed only recently, *Deinonychus* from Montana, U.S.A., and *Baryonyx* from Surrey, England, have proved the existence of spectacular new kinds of meat-eating dinosaurs in the Early Cretaceous, and both from areas that have been well searched by dinosaur hunters for over 100 years! These two new dinosaurs share the remarkable feature of a sickle-like slashing claw.

Deinonychus was first found in 1964 and, since then, more material has come to light. It was a lightweight animal, only 1.8 metres (6ft) long, with a powerful, high-sided skull, strong, long-fingered, grasping hands, and a stiff, rod-like tail for maintaining balance when the animal was running at high speed. The slashing claw was carried on the second toe from the inside. When walking or running, this claw was kept folded up, but it could swing down through more than 180° when required. *Deinonychus* was clearly agile enough to balance on one leg while kicking, or to leap through the air at a prey animal. It is likely that *Deinonychus* hunted the larger ornithopods in packs, as wild dogs do today. Other deinonychids include *Dromaeosaurus* from Canada, and *Velociraptor* from Mongolia. Both were discovered in the 1920s.

Right: The slashing claw of *Velociraptor mongoliensis* from the Late Cretaceous of Mongolia.

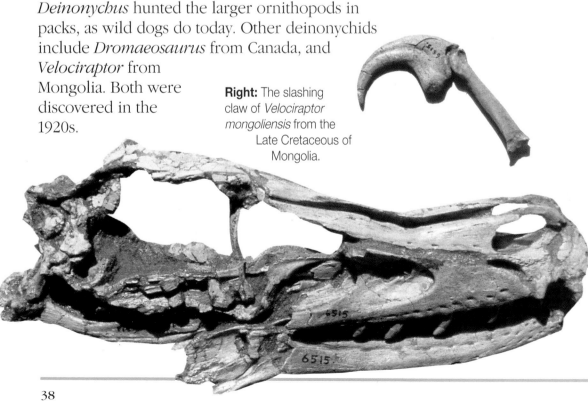

Left: The skull of *Velociraptor mongoliensis*, showing how lightly built it was. Note how few teeth there are, a typical feature of advanced theropods.

Baryonyx was found by an amateur collector in a brick pit near Ockley in Surrey in 1983. The sickle claw measures 30cm (12in) around the curve. *Baryonyx* was about 9 metres (30ft) long and it had a remarkable long crocodile-shaped skull. It is still not clear whether *Baryonyx* is a deinonychid or not, and indeed it is not certain whether the claw went on its hand or foot!

Below: Reconstructions of some sickle-clawed theropods. *Baryonyx* (top), with its long-snouted skull, is not closely related to the others, *Dromaeosaurus* (middle right), *Deinonychus* (bottom left) and *Velociraptor* (bottom right).

Above: The great slashing claw of *Baryonyx*, about 30cm (12in) long, compared with a pair of more normal claws which are rather smaller.

Left: Skeleton of the sickle-clawed *Dromaeosaurus*, from the late Cretaceous of Alberta, Canada. The sickle claw is rather small, but it would still have been an effective weapon of attack.

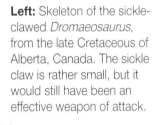

Above: Ockley Quarry, Surrey, England, site of the discovery of *Baryonyx* in 1983. The clay is quarried for brick-making, and bones are often found.

The Iguanodontids

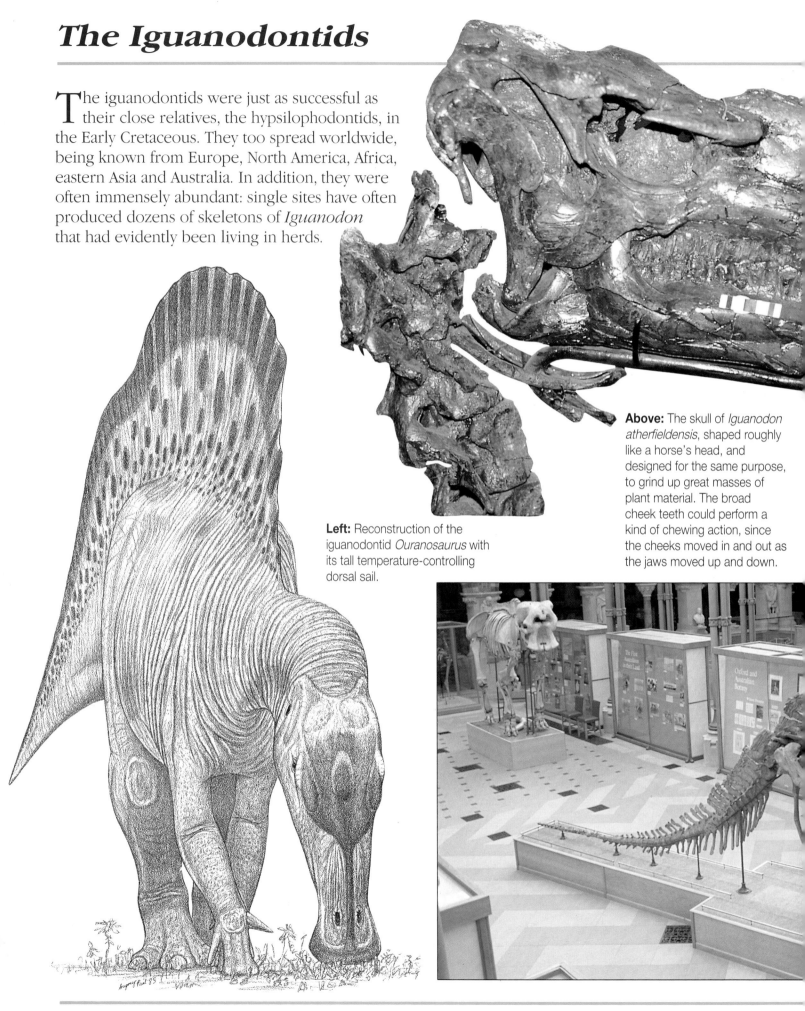

The iguanodontids were just as successful as their close relatives, the hypsilophodontids, in the Early Cretaceous. They too spread worldwide, being known from Europe, North America, Africa, eastern Asia and Australia. In addition, they were often immensely abundant: single sites have often produced dozens of skeletons of *Iguanodon* that had evidently been living in herds.

Above: The skull of *Iguanodon atherfieldensis*, shaped roughly like a horse's head, and designed for the same purpose, to grind up great masses of plant material. The broad cheek teeth could perform a kind of chewing action, since the cheeks moved in and out as the jaws moved up and down.

Left: Reconstruction of the iguanodontid *Ouranosaurus* with its tall temperature-controlling dorsal sail.

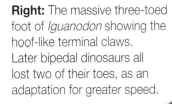

Right: The massive three-toed foot of *Iguanodon* showing the hoof-like terminal claws. Later bipedal dinosaurs all lost two of their toes, as an adaptation for greater speed.

Far right: The hand of *Iguanodon*. The three central fingers equipped with hooves show that the animal sometimes walked on all-fours. The thumb is a single great spike.

Left: Skeleton of *Iguanodon* in the Oxford University Museum. This rather "kangaroo-like" pose is not very lifelike. When the animal moved, it would have held its tail well clear of the ground.

Bones of *Iguanodon* itself were commonly found in southern England in the early nineteenth century, and it was named in 1825 by Dr Gideon Mantell, only the second dinosaur to be named (after *Megalosaurus*). Mantell's wife had apparently found two large teeth on a pile of road-mending stone in 1822. Gideon Mantell showed them to every expert he could find, and he received a wide range of identifications – anything from hippopotamuses to lizards. He then came across some limb bones and other elements, and eventually pronounced it a giant lizard. Since then, more complete specimens have been found in southern England, and in Belgium, north Germany and Spain. *Iguanodon* is now also known from Romania, North Africa, Mongolia and even North America (reported 1990).

The iguanodontids had the in-and-out chewing mechanism that was also developed by hypsilophodontids (see pages 36-37). They were large animals, 5 to 10 metres (16.5-33ft) long, and were generally bipedal, but could go on all-fours. They had hoof-like claws on most fingers, and a defensive spiked thumb claw. Relatives of *Iguanodon* included *Ouranosaurus* from the Sahara region of Africa, which had a "sail" running down its back, possibly a temperature-control mechanism, similar in function to the plates on the back of *Stegosaurus*.

New Armoured Dinosaurs

Armoured dinosaurs of the Jurassic were predominantly the stegosaurs, but this group declined during the Cretaceous. New armoured forms appeared, and many of these were foretastes of what was to follow in the Late Cretaceous.

The Wealden of southern England has produced evidence of two such groups: the ankylosaurs and the pachycephalosaurs. The ankylosaurs were commoner, being represented by several skeletons of two forms. *Hylaeosaurus* and *Polacanthus* were both 4 metres (13ft) long, and heavily armoured with long spines down the sides and on the tail, and thick bony plates set into the skin of the head, neck, body and tail. These ankylosaurs were relatively small compared to their descendants in the Late Cretaceous (see pages 54-55).

The second armoured dinosaur group from the Wealden, named *Yaverlandia*, is represented by much less impressive material – a fragment of skull roof. This fragment shows some bumps near its back margin, and it has been identified as the oldest pachycephalosaur, or bone-headed dinosaur. The group established itself properly in the Late Cretaceous (see pages 58-59).

A third armoured dinosaur group, the ceratopsians, also arose in the Early Cretaceous, but in Mongolia. The first ceratopsian, *Psittacosaurus*, had the body of an ornithopod like *Hypsilophodon* (see pages 36-37), but a strange beaked skull. There were no teeth at all in the front half of the jaws, and the bone here was probably covered by a horny beak in life. This first ceratopsian probably used its beak to nip off tough plants. It was the first member of a group that later became very important (see pages 60-61).

Right: Partial skeleton of *Psittacosaurus sinensis* from the mid Cretaceous of Mongolia. This shows the hip girdle (middle top), ribs, two thigh bones and a foot.

Left: Skull of the oldest bone-headed dinosaur, *Yaverlandia bitholus*, from the Early Cretaceous of the Isle of Wight. The bone over the top of the head is immensely thickened, and was probably used in head-butting.

Right: Complete skeleton of *Psittacosaurus sinensis* from Mongolia, showing the head (left), and the body extending to the right, including tail, arms and legs.

Right: Digging fossils in Mongolia, the source of many Cretaceous armoured dinosaurs. This locality, called Khongil, has produced skeletons of ankylosaurs, which were highly armoured dinosaurs.

5 The Late Cretaceous World

Dinosaurs of the Late Cretaceous are much better known than those of the Early Cretaceous, and they are represented by large assemblages in all parts of the world. In addition, the dinosaurs of the Late Cretaceous were more varied and abundant than at any other time. As many as fifteen or twenty species lived side by side in any area at the same time, compared to fewer than ten previously. Moreover, the total range of dinosaur species worldwide had never been higher than in the Late Cretaceous.

The classic areas for Late Cretaceous dinosaurs are in North America (especially Alberta and Montana) and in eastern Asia (Mongolia, China). The Late Cretaceous beds of midwestern North America were explored by the great collectors last century, and they named many of the most famous dinosaurs from them: *Tyrannosaurus*, *Triceratops*, *Anatosaurus*, *Corythosaurus*, *Ankylosaurus* and so on.

Above: The Ikh-Shunkht locality in Mongolia, a Late Cretaceous dinosaur site which has produced many types of egg shells and nests of eggs, excavated by Polish scientists.

Below: Dinosaur badlands: Late Cretaceous sediments of Alberta, Canada. The sediments are mudstones and sandstones laid down in ancient rivers.

Right: A Late Cretaceous scene in Alberta, Canada. A juvenile and an adult *Dromaeosaurus* feed on a horned dinosaur, probably killed by a tyrannosaur.

The Late Cretaceous of Mongolia was explored next, playing host to expeditions from the American Museum in the 1920s, from Moscow in the 1940s and 1950s, and from Poland in the 1960s and 1970s. The dinosaurs from Mongolia matched species for species those from North America: they were very similar, but not quite the same. In both countries, the main plant-eaters were duck-billed ornithopods (see pages 56-57), horned ceratopsians (see pages 60-61), armoured ankylosaurs (see pages 54-55), and the bone-headed pachycephalosaurs (see pages 58-59). Meat-eaters included the small ostrich dinosaurs (see pages 46-47), some odd theropods (see pages 48-49), and the giant tyrannosaurs (see pages 50-51). The only group missing in North America and Mongolia was the sauropods, known in the Late Cretaceous from other regions (see pages 52-53).

Above: Late Cretaceous sediments in Texas, U.S.A., the Javelina Formation, source of the world's largest flying reptile, *Quetzalcoatlus*.

Below: A typical scene of life 70 million years ago, in the Late Cretaceous of Alberta: *Albertosaurus* is feeding on the carcass of a ceratopsian.

The Ostrich Dinosaurs

Two remarkable groups of meat-eating theropods rose to importance in the Late Cretaceous, the ornithomimosaurs and the oviraptorosaurs. Both are distinguished by their total lack of teeth, a remarkable state of affairs in dinosaurs that apparently fed on meat! However, birds like eagles and vultures seem to manage perfectly well without teeth today, so this may not be so unusual.

The ornithomimosaurs (the name means "bird mimic reptiles") are known only from North America and Mongolia. They were generally 3 to 4 metres (10-13ft) in length, but lightweight since most of this length comprised a long tail and neck. *Ornithomimus*, from Colorado, Montana and Alberta, was first discovered in 1889, but a complete skeleton was found only in 1917. This revealed it as an ostrich-like animal, with a small, bird-like head on a long flexible neck, a rounded body and long slender legs. It was clear that *Ornithomimus* probably ran like an ostrich, with great rapid strides, and may have been able to achieve a speed of 65km/h (40mph). It had a long tail (for balancing) and powerful long-fingered hands, which may have been used for grasping prey items, or even eggs. Other ornithomimosaurs are *Struthiomimus* and *Dromiceomimus*.

The oviraptorosaurs ("egg-stealing reptiles") are known only by *Oviraptor* from the Late Cretaceous of Mongolia, a possible relative of the ornithomimosaurs. *Oviraptor* is also toothless, but the skull is very oddly shaped. It is short and very high, and the lower jaw does not meet the upper for much of its length. There is great variety in the skull shapes too, some having bumps over the nose, others having sizable crests. The rest of the skeleton is poorly known. A possible oviraptorosaur from North America may be *Caenagnathus*, a dinosaur named long ago on the basis of a strange lower jaw.

Right: Skeleton of *Struthiomimus* in the Royal Tyrrell Museum of Palaeontology, Drumheller, Alberta, just as it was found. The head is bent back by drying of the carcass.

Below: Skull of the ostrich dinosaur *Struthiomimus* showing the complete absence of teeth. The skull is lightly built, as in a bird, and the long snout was covered by a horny beak.

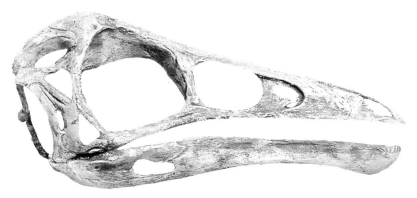

Left: Model of the ostrich dinosaur *Struthiomimus* showing its lightweight body, long neck and small, intelligent, bird-like head.

Above: Skull of *Dromiceomimus.* The huge eye socket is set well back in the head, and it is evidence for powerful eyesight.

Above: Excavating the ostrich dinosaur *Gallimimus* at Altan Ula, Mongolia, in 1971. The long slender bones of the limbs may be seen clearly.

Below: Skull of *Oviraptor* from Khermeen Tsav, Mongolia, excavated in 1971. The snout, facing right, is short and the jaws are deep and toothless.

Strange Claws and Teeth

The Late Cretaceous is remarkable for its crop of weird and wonderful theropods – meat-eaters of all shapes and sizes that cannot be classified at all. There are giant unidentifiable pairs of arms, huge claws, bird-like forms and some that might not even be theropods!

The giant arms of a creature named *Deinocheirus* were found in Mongolia in the 1960s. Each arm is 2.6 metres (8.5ft) long, and each hand has three fingers. Each of these bears a claw about 25cm (10in) long. If the arms are in proportion to those of other theropods, they must have come from an unbelievably huge meat-eater. They resemble those of an ornithomimosaur most closely, but they are three times larger than those of the largest ostrich dinosaur!

In 1981, a slender bird-like theropod from Mongolia was named as *Avimimus*. This 1.5 metre- (5ft-) long animal had some bird-like features in the shoulder region and in the arm bones. One of these had a low bone ridge in just the place where the big flight feathers of birds attach. Could this have been a feathered dinosaur?

The giant claws came from the Late Cretaceous of Argentina and Mongolia. *Noasaurus* from Argentina is known from a partial skull and a slashing claw, rather like that of *Deinonychus*, but different enough to suggest that the two were not related. The Mongolian "claws" is *Therizinosaurus*

Below: Reconstruction of the astonishing long-clawed *Therizinosaurus* (right) facing an attack from the tyrannosaur *Tarbosaurus*, 75 million years ago in Mongolia. Only the arms of *Therizino-saurus* are known.

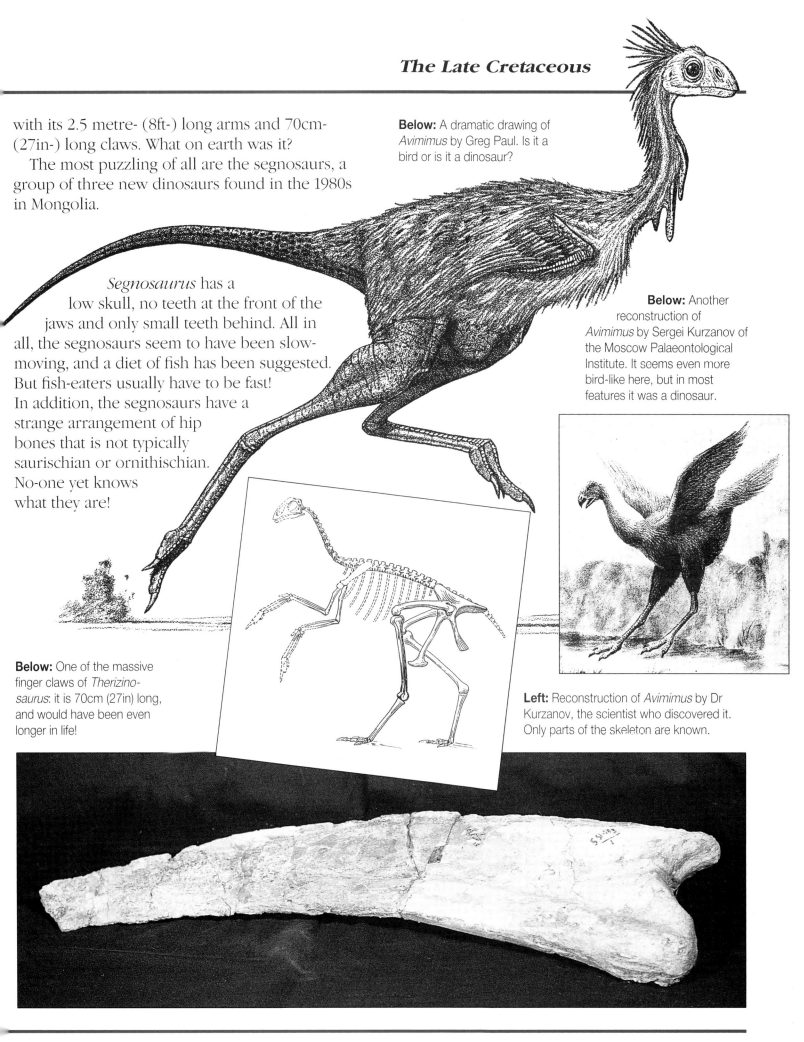

with its 2.5 metre- (8ft-) long arms and 70cm-
(27in-) long claws. What on earth was it?

The most puzzling of all are the segnosaurs, a
group of three new dinosaurs found in the 1980s
in Mongolia.

Below: A dramatic drawing of
Avimimus by Greg Paul. Is it a
bird or is it a dinosaur?

Segnosaurus has a
low skull, no teeth at the front of the
jaws and only small teeth behind. All in
all, the segnosaurs seem to have been slow-
moving, and a diet of fish has been suggested.
But fish-eaters usually have to be fast!
In addition, the segnosaurs have a
strange arrangement of hip
bones that is not typically
saurischian or ornithischian.
No-one yet knows
what they are!

Below: Another
reconstruction of
Avimimus by Sergei Kurzanov of
the Moscow Palaeontological
Institute. It seems even more
bird-like here, but in most
features it was a dinosaur.

Below: One of the massive
finger claws of *Therizino-
saurus*: it is 70cm (27in) long,
and would have been even
longer in life!

Left: Reconstruction of *Avimimus* by Dr
Kurzanov, the scientist who discovered it.
Only parts of the skeleton are known.

The Largest Meat-Eaters

Large theropods arose in the Middle Jurassic, but the group reached its pinnacle much later, in the Late Cretaceous, with the tyrannosaurs. These included the biggest meat-eating land animal of all time, *Tyrannosaurus rex*, as well as numerous other similar large carnivorous dinosaurs from North America, Mongolia, Russia, India and South America.

Tyrannosaurus rex was named in 1905 on the basis of an incomplete skeleton from Montana. Further skeletons were found soon after and they gave a fairly complete picture of this animal. It is a remarkable fact, however, that no-one has ever found a complete skeleton of *Tyrannosaurus*, and there are only a couple of skulls known (despite the hundreds of casts to be seen all over the world!).

Left: Skeleton of the giant tyrannosaur *Tarbosaurus* from Mongolia, mounted in the Palaeontological Institute, Moscow. The head is like *Tyrannosaurus*.

Above: Two friendly specimens of *Dryptosaurus* engage in some horseplay in the Late Cretaceous of North America. This classic painting by Charles Knight dates from 1906.

Below: *Albertosaurus*, a lightweight tyrannosaur from the Late Cretaceous of Alberta, Canada, a skeleton mounted in the Royal Tyrrell Museum of Palaeontology, Drumheller, Alberta, Canada.

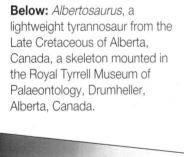

Below: Skeleton of *Tyrannosaurus rex*, possible the most famous dinosaur of all, in a half mount as it used to be seen in the Natural History Museum, London.

Above: Tyrannosaurs on the attack: *Daspletosaurus* (left) and *Tyrannosaurus* (middle) from North America, and *Tarbosaurus* (right) from Mongolia. All had massive heads, long teeth and powerful three-toed feet for holding prey.

Tyrannosaurus was 14 metres (46ft) long, and stood 5 to 6 metres (16.5-19.5ft) high. Its mouth was lined with teeth up to 18cm (7in) long (each was the size of a carving knife), and its gape was large enough to engulf a child whole. Indeed, *Tyrannosaurus* was so large that a fully-grown man would only have reached up to its knee. Clearly, *Tyrannosaurus* could have attacked successfully any of the plant-eaters of its day.

The other tyrannosaurs include a nearly identical large form from Mongolia, *Tarbosaurus*, as well as smaller relatives from North America such as *Albertosaurus* and *Daspletosaurus*. The tyrannosaurs from other parts of the world are still too poorly known to be sure of their appearance and relationships.

51

The Last Sauropods

The sauropods enjoyed their heyday in the Late Jurassic, when diplodocids, camarasaurids and brachiosaurids spread worldwide, and were the commonest plant-eaters. The sauropods declined in significance in the Cretaceous, although some important groups lived on, especially in southern continents.

One or two Early Cretaceous sauropods are known: for example, a diplodocid and a brachiosaurid are known from odd bones found in the Wealden of England, along with the much commoner ornithopods.

A diplodocid called *Nemegtosaurus* lived in Mongolia in the Late Cretaceous. It is known only from its skull, which is not very different from that of the Late Jurassic *Diplodocus*. A headless skeleton, also from Mongolia, has been named *Opisthocoelicaudia*; tempting as it might seem, this is not the skeleton belonging to the skull of *Nemegtosaurus* since *Opisthocoelicaudia* seems to belong to the camarasaurid family.

Below: A large humerus (upper arm bone) of a sauropod is uncovered from Early Cretaceous sediments on the Isle of Wight. These giants were rare in the Cretaceous.

Above: Excavating a sauropod limb bone from the Early Cretaceous of the Isle of Wight. Such huge bones require as much care as smaller ones since they can readily break.

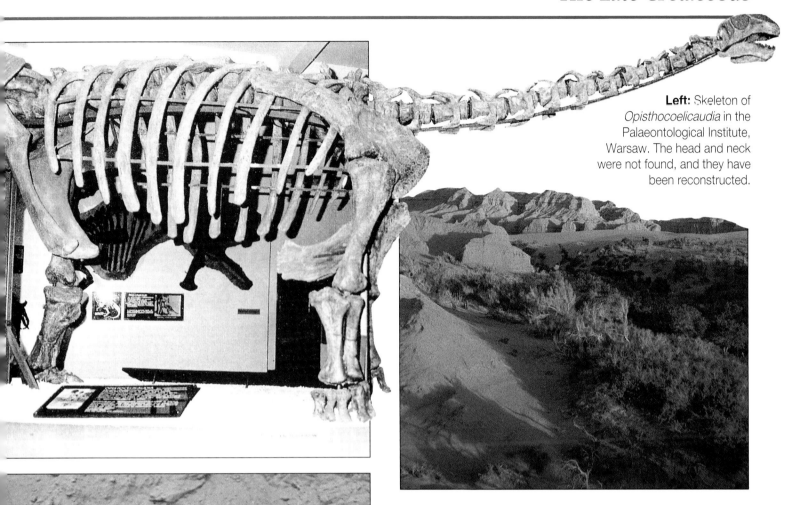

Left: Skeleton of *Opisthocoelicaudia* in the Palaeontological Institute, Warsaw. The head and neck were not found, and they have been reconstructed.

Left: A team of Polish palaeontologists excavates the skeleton of the Late Cretaceous sauropod *Opisthocoelicaudia* at Altan Ula, Mongolia, in 1970.

Above: The dinosaur locality Khermeen Tsav in Mongolia, site of many dinosaur finds by Polish and Russian palaeontological teams.

Opisthocoelicaudia has massive, pillar-like leg bones, and an unusual tail that does not bend downwards. It actually sticks out backwards and a little upwards. It has been suggested that the tail may have had a specialised use as a support for when *Opisthocoelicaudia* reared up on its hind legs to feed: it might have sat on a sort of tripod made from its hind legs and the tail.

The main Late Cretaceous sauropods were the titanosaurids, like *Saltasaurus* from Argentina, *Titanosaurus* from Argentina and India, and *Hypselosaurus* from France. *Saltasaurus* is unusual in having rounded armour plates set in the skin of its back. *Titanosaurus* is very similar. *Hypselosaurus* is interesting because several sites in southern France have yielded abundant fragments of its eggshells.

The Ankylosaurs

Ankylosaurs were heavy, four-legged, armoured dinosaurs known first in the Early Cretaceous (see pages 42-43), but they became more common in the Late Cretaceous. Some, like *Nodosaurus* from midwestern North America, were rather like the Early Cretaceous forms, with a covering of armour plates over the back, the tail and the head, and with a flexible pointed tail.

A second ankylosaur group spread in the Late Cretaceous. These new forms had broad triangular heads that were as broad as they were long, and they sported remarkable bony tail clubs. The largest ankylosaurs, *Euoplocephalus* (6 metres, 20ft long) and *Ankylosaurus* (10 metres, 33ft long) from North America, and *Talarurus* (5 to 7 metres, 16.5-23ft long) from Mongolia, were the size and weight of small armoured tanks. Their skulls were covered with a "second skull", an outer plating of extra bones that formed in the skin, and served to protect the head. *Euoplocephalus* even had a bony eyelid cover to protect its eye! These ankylosaurs also had horns at the back of the skull.

The body and tail were covered with rings of bony plates set in the skin, with odd bony spines scattered here and there. The most striking feature is the tail club. The last few bones of the tail were fused together, and they combined with some bones formed in the skin to make a rounded double club.

Above: Model of the ankylosaur *Edmontonia*, showing the armour set into the skin of its back and head, and the sharp spines.

The tail in front of the club was flexible and no doubt this allowed the club to be swung forceably at any predator that was trying to attack.

Right: Tail club of *Euoplocephalus*, a large ankylosaur. The tail club is made from a fused mass of bone, including the last tail vertebrae.

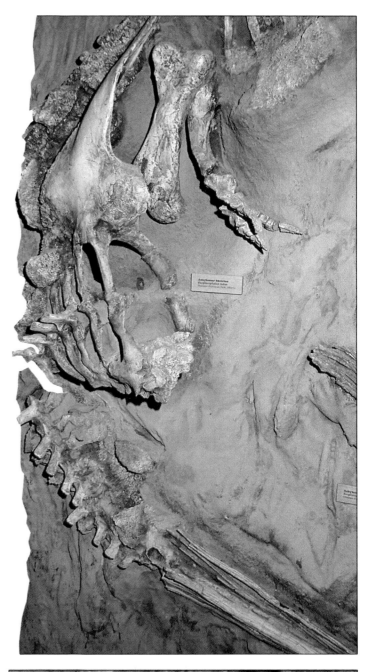

Right: Partial skeleton of the ankylosaur *Euoplocephalus*, showing the backbone, hip bones (top left), hind limb (top right) and scattered ribs.

Right: Uncovering the ankylosaur *Saichania* from Late Cretaceous sediments at Khulsan, Mongolia. The massive armoured head faces to the right: this picture reinforces the fact that most ankylosaurs were large animals.

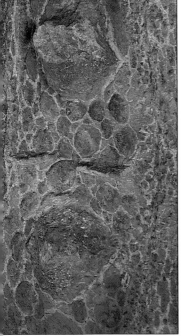

Left: The preserved skin of the ankylosaur *Scolosaurus*, showing the large and small nodules and plates of bone which formed a kind of rigid chain mail over the body.

The Duckbills

The ultimate flowering of the ornithopods took place in the Late Cretaceous when the hadrosaurs, or duckbilled dinosaurs, were prominent. These built on the success of their ancestors, the Late Jurassic and Early Cretaceous hypsilophodontids and iguanodontids. The duckbills include dozens of species worldwide, but known best from North America and Mongolia. Often six or seven species lived side by side with one another in any one place.

Most of the duckbills had strange crests on their heads: a high crest like a dinner plate in *Corythosaurus*, a long schnorkel-like structure in *Parasaurolophus*, a forward-pointing spine in *Tsintaosaurus*, and a low inflated area on top of the snout in *Edmontosaurus* and *Anatosaurus*. At first, it was thought that the duckbills lived all of their time in water (after all, they have duck bills!) and that the crests were like aqualungs, for storing air while they dived. However, the duckbills were far too big to be sustained by the amount of air that could be stored in the crest.

The crests are hollow inside, and the breathing tubes pass from the nostrils up through the crest and down the throat. Experiments with models have shown that when a duckbill breathed out, it made a honking or whistling sound through the tubes in the crest. Each crest made a different sound, just like the wind instruments in an orchestra. Males and females and juveniles had different crests, and we can imagine the Late Cretaceous forests reverberating to a cacophony of honks and whistles as babies tried to find their mothers, males and females tried to find mates of the correct species, and others made threatening displays!

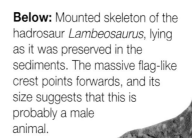

Below: Mounted skeleton of the hadrosaur *Lambeosaurus*, lying as it was preserved in the sediments. The massive flag-like crest points forwards, and its size suggests that this is probably a male animal.

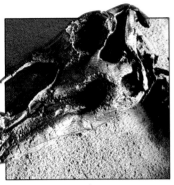

Above: Skull of a crestless hadrosaur, *Edmontosaurus altispinus*. The front of the snout was toothless, but the bony pads there grasped leaves.

Left: One of the most striking of the hadrosaurs, *Parasaurolophus*, with its long, tubular head crest. It is clear why many thought that the crest was a schnorkel, but is has no hole at the end, and so could not have been used in that way.

Above: *Lambeosaurus* (left) and *Corythosaurus* (right) and the heads of *Hadrosaurus* (top left), *Tsintaosaurus* (top middle), *Parasaurolophus* (top right), *Edmontosaurus* (middle left), and *Saurolophus* (middle).

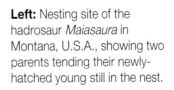

Left: Nesting site of the hadrosaur *Maiasaura* in Montana, U.S.A., showing two parents tending their newly-hatched young still in the nest.

Above: Skull of *Corythosaurus casuarius,* bearing a rounded plate-like crest which is made from the bones on top of the snout which grow up and back.

The Boneheads

The pachycephalosaurs are another essentially Late Cretaceous group, but they had an obscure ancestor in the Early Cretaceous of southern England (see pages 42-43). They are known best from Mongolia and North America. The oddest feature of the pachycephalosaurs is the enormously thickened skull roof – in some species up to 25cm (10in) of solid bone! This characteristic gave rise to their name; pachycephalosaur means "thick headed reptile". Most pachycephalosaur fossils are actually just the thickened head shield, and very few are known from more complete remains.

Two pachycephalosaurs were found earlier this century in Alberta and Montana, *Stegoceras* and *Pachycephalosaurus*, the first one being 2 metres (6.5ft) in length, and the second 8 metres (26ft). At first, only isolated bits and pieces of their skulls came to light, but subsequently one or two skeletons were also found. These showed that the pachycephalosaurs were bipedal, having roughly the body outline of a typical ornithopod, but the head bore a raised dome. In *Stegoceras* the dome was high and rose over the whole snout, while in *Pachycephalosaurus* the dome rose over the back half of the skull, which was also equipped with low bony spines behind the head and on the snout.

More recent finds from Mongolia have shown that the pachycephalosaurs had reinforced hip bones, powerful backbones, and strengthened bones in the neck. These features, and the thick skull, were a mystery until it was suggested that the pachycephalosaurs head-butted one another in displays to establish territorial dominance, or to attract mates, just as wild sheep and goats do today. The thickened skull roof protected the pachycephalosaur's brain (small as it was!) against enormous impacts as they clashed, and the force of the blow travelled down the neck, along a specially strengthened backbone, to be finally absorbed around the hip region.

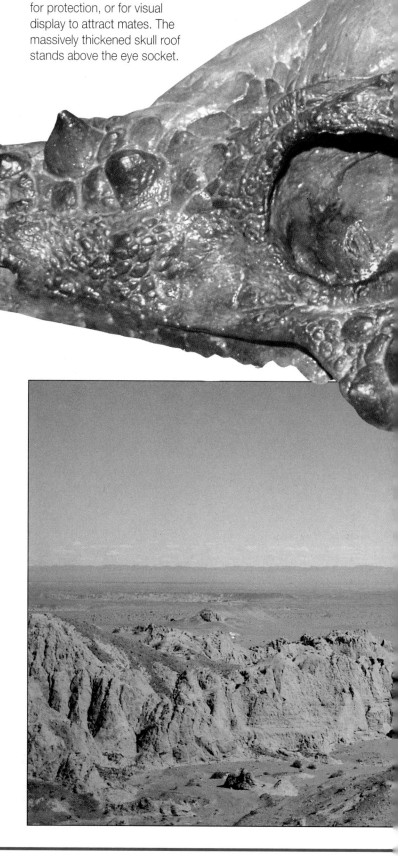

Right: Skull of *Pachycephalosaurus*, one of the best-known boneheaded dinosaurs. The knobbly spines may have been for protection, or for visual display to attract mates. The massively thickened skull roof stands above the eye socket.

Below: Model of the bonehead *Stegoceras* sprinting through the undergrowth in Alberta, Canada. The thickened skull runs to the tip of the snout.

Above: Another view of the Khulsan locality, Mongolia, one of several sites in the Late Cretaceous of the area that produced pachycephalosaur remains.

Left: The Khulsan locality in Mongolia, site of various fossil finds, including pachycephalosaur skeletons.

The Horned Dinosaurs

Close relatives of the pachycephalosaurs, and nearly as common as the duckbills in the Late Cretaceous, were the ceratopsians, or horned dinosaurs. They arose from ancestors like the bipedal *Psittacosaurus* (see pages 42-43), but soon all became four-legged animals. The second ceratopsian in time, after *Psittacosaurus*, was *Protoceratops*, also from Mongolia. This small, 1.8 metre- (6ft-) long, animal was found by the 1920s' American Museum expedition to Mongolia when clutches of its eggs were also uncovered. *Protoceratops* has a beaked snout, a low shield of bone over its neck region, and a thickened area on top of the snout. The eggs were laid in circles of ten or twenty, and buried in the warm sand. Some of the nests even had babies preserved round about.

Later ceratopsians all had the neck frill, really an outgrowth from the normal bones around the back of the skull. The frill adopted all kinds of shapes in the different species, being rounded with its edge covered with bony nodules in *Triceratops*, bearing numerous long spines in *Styracosaurus*, and adding hugely to the skull length in *Torosaurus*. Indeed, one specimen of *Torosaurus* has a skull 2.6 metres (8.5ft) long, in an animal that was 7.6 metres (25ft) in total length. This is the largest head of any land animal.

The ceratopsians also generally had a nose horn like a rhinoceros today, and sometimes other facial horns. *Protoceratops* had a raised area on the snout, where all later forms had a long nose horn. *Triceratops* also had a long horn over each eye, as did *Torosaurus*.

The neck frill would have protected the neck area from attack, and it was also a place for the jaw muscles to attach. The horns on the face must have been useful in defence also. It is possible that herds of ceratopsians would form a circle around their young, heads and horns facing out, to deter any *Tyrannosaurus* from coming too close.

Right: The horned dinosaur, *Triceratops horridus*, showing its characteristic three horns, one on the snout and a long one over each eye socket. The broad hands and feet bear hooves instead of claws, and the limb structure shows that these large ceratopsians could gallop fast.

Below: Model of baby *Protoceratops* hatching from their eggs. Numerous eggs, nests and juveniles of this species have been found.

Above: Skull of the early ceratopsian *Protoceratops.* It has the characteristic neck frill, but no horn on its snout, just a bone thickening.

Right: Typical ceratopsians: *Torosaurus* (top left), *Styracosaurus* (top right) *Triceratops* (bottom left), *Centrosaurus* (bottom right) and *Protoceratops* (middle).

Below: *Chasmosaurus*, a ceratopsian from Alberta, Canada. The great length of neck frill, and the massive weight of the head are evident, and these features required powerful neck muscles.

Why Did They Die Out?

The last dinosaurs disappeared 65 million years ago. For a long time the explanation seemed simple. The dinosaurs had been around for long enough, and they were lumbering great monsters that were not clever enough to survive. They just died off in the face of competition from the hairy, warm-blooded mammals that were to replace them.

However, things were not so simple. First, the dinosaurs were highly successful animals, especially in the Late Cretaceous. Indeed, they had never been so varied and so plentiful. Second, there is no sign of a long-term decline; they lived right up to the end, with the last-gasp dinosaurs being such "successful" forms as *Triceratops*, *Tyrannosaurus* and various duckbills.

There are now two broad theories for what happened. One is that climates became cooler, and the dinosaurs dwindled away over several million years as their warm habitats disappeared. This long-term kind of view can also explain the mass extinction of other kinds of animals at the same time. The flying pterosaurs and the great sea reptiles all disappeared about then, as did many other sea creatures.

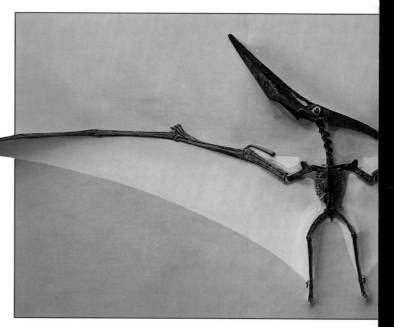

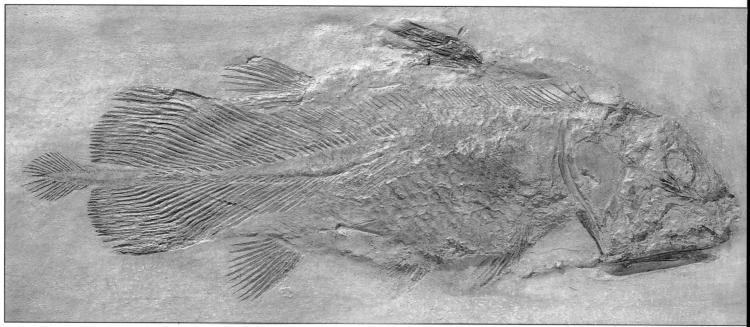

Left: Skeleton of an ichthyosaur, a dolphin-like marine reptile group that died out in the Late Cretaceous, but sometime before the demise of the dinosaurs.

Below: Underside of the shell of the turtle *Dinochelys*, showing the bony plastron in the middle, the rim of the upper shell, the carapace round the edges and a partial limb. The turtles were able to survive the mass extinction event 65 million years ago unscathed.

The other view is that there was a great catastrophe. An asteroid may have hit the Earth and sent a vast cloud of shattered rocks and dust high into the atmosphere, where it circled the Earth, blacked out the Sun, and caused a long spell of darkness and great cold. Many plants and animals on land and in the seas would have perished, and these victims included the dinosaurs.

At the moment, it is hard to decide between these theories. However, one of the real mysteries is why so many animals survived unaffected. Fishes, frogs, turtles, lizards, crocodiles, birds and mammals all lived on. No theory can yet explain why they survived and the dinosaurs and others disappeared.

Above: Model of the giant pterosaur *Pteranodon*, one of the last survivors of its group. The pterosaurs ruled the skies for 160 million years, the same span of time as the dinosaurs, but they were eventually replaced by birds.

Left: The coelacanth *Holophagus penicillata*, from the Jurassic. It was once thought that these unusual fishes had died out during the Jurassic or Cretaceous, until a living coelacanth, *Latimeria*, was fished up off Africa in 1938.

Below: The shell of a modern giant land tortoise, with the arched carapace above and the plastron below. Large turtles and large crocodiles seemed to survive the mass extinction event, so it was not simply size that finished the dinosaurs.

Picture Credits

The publishers would like to thank the many palaeontologists, private collectors, museums and picture agencies who supplied the illustrations reproduced in this book. Special thanks are due to John Sibbick who created artwork specifically for the book, and to the custodians of the Tyrrell Museum of Palaeontology, Drumheller, Alberta, who so generously supplied many of the illustrations reproduced here. Pictures are credited by page number.

Bayerische Staatssammlung für Paläontologie und historische Geologie: 32 lower. **Michael Benton:** 7 upper, 14, 14-15, 15 upper, 36-37, 38-39 lower, 39 upper. **The Bettmann Archive:** 50 upper right. **Peter Bull Studio:** 4-5 artwork, 11 artwork, 15 artwork. **City of Bristol Museum and Art Gallery:** 21 top right. **Professor E. H. Colbert, Museum of Northern Arizona:** 9 middle and lower, 17 lower, 20 lower left, 21 lower left, 25 lower right. **Field Museum of Natural History, Chicago:** 61 upper left. **Chris Gow, University of the Witwatersrand:** 12 upper and lower, 13 lower. **Stephen Hutt:** 34 lower left and right, 37 upper left and right, 52 upper and lower. **Imitor:** 4-5, 5 lower, 8 upper, 10 upper, 18 lower, 26 lower, 27 upper right, 32 upper, 33 lower, 34-35, 35, 41 upper middle and right, 42, 50-51, 54-55, 60 lower left, 62, 62-63 upper and middle, 63 lower. **Institute of Palaeobiology, Warsaw (W. Skarzynski):** 47 middle right and lower right, 52-53, 53 upper left, 55 lower right. **S. M. Kurzanov, Palaeontological Institute, Moscow:** 43, 44 upper, 49 middle, middle right, and lower, 50 middle, 53 upper right, 58-59 lower, 59 upper. **Leicestershire Museums, Arts and Records Service:** 6, 25 lower left.

Makoto Manabe: 28 middle, 42-43 upper and lower. **James H. Madsen Jr., Dinolab:** 4 upper, 23 middle and lower. **Museum of Northern Arizona:** 21 middle. **National Museum of Ottawa:** 57 upper left. **Gregory S. Paul:** 13 upper, 22-23 upper, 28 lower, 40, 48, 49 upper. **Peabody Museum of Natural History, Yale University:** 19 lower. **John Sibbick:** 2-3, 6-7, 8 lower, 27 lower, 29 upper, 39 lower, 51 upper, 57 upper right, 61 upper right. **South African Museum:** 10 lower, 10-11, 12-13. **Staatliches Museum für Naturkunde in Stuttgart:** 7 upper, 16 upper and lower, 17 upper. **Tyrrell Museum of Palaeontology (photographs by Colin Orthner):** title page, 5 upper, 9 upper, 11, 20-21, 24 upper, 27 upper left, 28-29, 30-31 lower, 31 middle, 38 lower, 38-39 upper, 44 middle and lower, 44-45 lower (Vladimir Krb), 46, 46-47, 47 upper left and right, 50 lower left, 54, 54-55 upper, 55 upper, 56, 56-47 middle and lower, 58-59 upper, 59 lower, 60-61, 61 lower. **Universität Tübingen:** 17 middle. **University Museum, Oxford:** 30 lower left, 30-31 upper, 31 lower, 40-41 lower. **U.S. Department of the Interior, National Park Service, Dinosaur National Monument:** 18 lower, 18-19, 19 upper, 23-23 lower, 24 lower, 28 upper, 63 upper. **David Weishampel:** 31 upper, 36 lower, 37 lower, 40-41 upper, 57 lower right. **Peter Wellnhofer:** 25 upper, 33 upper, 44-45 upper.

Cover pictures: Vladimir Krb/Tyrrell Museum of Palaeontology (front); John Sibbick (back, artwork); Tyrrell Museum of Palaeontology (back, skeleton and backdrops).

Index